CW00434199

TREATY OF THE GREAT KING

The Covenant Structure of Deuteronomy:
Studies and Commentary

TREATY OF THE GREAT KING

GREAT KING

The Covenant Structure of Deuteronomy:
Studies and Commentary

by

MEREDITH G. KLINE

Associate Professor of Old Testament
Westminster Theological Seminary, Philadelphia

WIPF & STOCK · Eugene, Oregon

Wipf and Stock Publishers
199 W 8th Ave, Suite 3
Eugene, OR 97401

Treaty of the Great King
The Covenant Structure of Deuteronomy: Studies and Commentary
By Kline, Meredith G.
Copyright©1963 by Kline, Meredith G.
ISBN 13: 978-1-61097-698-5
Publication date 1/3/2012
Previously published by Wm. B. Eerdmans, 1963

*This book
is dedicated to
the memory of*
NED B. STONEHOUSE

PREFACE

The rediscovery of treaties of the great kings of Near Eastern antiquity has been widely exploited by biblical scholarship in the last few years. It has been generally recognized that certain adjustments are required in the negatitve judgments which control modern studies in the area of Old Testament history and higher criticism, but it does not yet seem to have been appreciated that in these treaties the modern biblical critic has a tiger by the tail. The significance of the treaties for subjects like the beginnings of the canon of Scripture and the authenticity of the Pentateuch as well as the historicity of various covenants recorded in the Bible can hardly be overestimated. An attempt is made here to trace the relevance of the recovery of the treaty form for our understanding of the nature of the Decalogue and Deuteronomy, with particular reference to the current phase of Old Testament higher criticism.

If not as much in the foreground as the apologetic design in the present volume, the biblical theological aspects of these investigations nevertheless occupy a more central position in the interests of the author. It is intended that the studies should serve as a preliminary probe, preparing for a more systematic exploration of the history of the revelation of God's covenants with man.

The two chapters of Part I first appeared as articles in the *Westminster Theological Journal* in the issues of May, 1960 (Vol. XXII, No. 2) and November, 1960 (Vol. XXIII, No. 1). The original articles have been somewhat modified, particularly to take account of important, more recent developments. The brief commentary on Deuteronomy found in Part II is substantially that which I contributed to *The Wycliffe Bible Commentary* (Chicago: Moody Press. 1962). The purposes and policies of that volume naturally determined the general nature and scope of the treatment of the individual contributions, as well as matters like the system of transliteration of Hebrew and Greek words and the form of biblical quotations. The latter are from the Authorized Version unless otherwise noted.

Although this combination of materials is somewhat unusual, it was felt that the two parts satisfactorily supplemented each other in their common unfolding of the suzerainty treaty pattern as found in the Mosaic covenants. By means of the commentary the results of the studies of Part I may be made more serviceable to the immediate needs of the preacher and teacher of the Bible; yet, because of the commentary's primary and constant concern with questions of structure, whether the pattern of the treaty as a whole or the arrangement of materials within subordinate sections like the stipulations, it is hoped that it may in this respect at least serve those with more specialized interests.

The opportunity is welcomed to acknowledge with deep appreciation the generosity of the Moody Press and also the kindness of the editors of the *Westminster Theological Journal* in granting republication privileges. My thanks are also due to Miss Dorothy Newkirk for her services in preparing the typescript. And to the publishers, the Wm. B. Eerdmans Publishing Company, belongs my sincere gratitude for their bravery in accepting the work of a new author and for their many subsequent courtesies.

* * * * *

Within the month Westminster Theological Seminary has suffered great loss in the departure of Professor Ned B. Stonehouse to be at home with the Lord. We younger members of the faculty first knew him as teacher and when it became our further privilege to serve with him as colleagues we continued to seek and treasure his wise counsel on many matters, personal and professional. How fresh the memory of the warm encouragement which Dr. Stonehouse added to his advice when I sought his judgment on the publication of this my first book.

"So teach us to number our days, that we may get us a heart of wisdom."

—MEREDITH G. KLINE

Westminster Theological Seminary,
December 15, 1962

CONTENTS

Part I

THE TREATY FORM OF
THE DECALOGUE AND DEUTERONOMY

1. The Two Tables of the Covenant

"And he declared unto you his covenant, which he commanded you to perform, even ten commandments; and he wrote them upon two tables of stone" (Deut. 4:13). It has been commonly assumed that each of the stone tables contained but a part of the total revelation proclaimed by the voice of God out of the fiery theophany on Sinai. Only the subordinate question of the dividing point between the "first and second tables" has occasioned disagreement.[1] A re-examination of the biblical data, however, particularly in the light of extra-biblical parallels, suggests a radically new interpretation of the formal nature of the two stone tables, the importance of which will be found to lie primarily in the fresh perspective it lends to our understanding of the divine oracle engraved upon them.

Attention is being directed more and more in recent years to the remarkable resemblance between God's covenant with Israel and the suzerainty (also called vassal) type of international treaty found in the ancient Near East.[2] Similarities have been

1. The dominant opinion has been that the "second table" opens with the fifth commandment, but Jews usually count the fifth commandment as the last in the "first table", filial reverence being regarded as a religious duty. (Here and elsewhere in this chapter the designation of specific commandments is based on the common Protestant enumeration.) For a different ancient Jewish opinion anticipating the conclusion of the present study see *Midrash Rabbah*, XLVII, 6.

2. See G. E. Mendenhall, "Covenant Forms in Israelite Tradition," *The Biblical Archaeologist, XVII* (1954) 3, pp. 50-76; this was republished in *Law and Covenant in Israel and the Ancient Near East*, 1955. D. J. Wiseman had previously read a paper on some of the parallels to the Society for Old Testament Studies (Jan. 1948). See now K. Baltzer, *Das Bundesformular. Seine Ursprung und seine Verwendung im AT* (Wiss. Monogr. 2. A. und N.T., 4), Neukirchen, 1960. There are references to such international treaties in the third millennium B.C. Actual treaty texts of the New Hittite Empire in the full classic form of the mid-second millennium B.C. were discovered almost forty years ago in the archives of ancient Hattusa. The evidence for this period has been supplemented by a few treaty fragments found at Ugarit. Other recent finds bring the evidence for vassal treaties down into the first half of the first millennium B.C. Most significant are the three Aramaic inscriptions from Sefireh and the Assyrian treaties of Esarhaddon found at Nimrud.

13

discovered in the areas of the documents, the ceremonies of ratification, the modes of administration, and, most basically of course, the suzerain-servant relationship itself. On the biblical side the resemblance is most apparent in the accounts of the theocratic covenant as instituted through the mediatorship of Moses at Sinai and as later renewed under both Moses and Joshua. Of most interest for the subject of this chapter is the fact that the pattern of the suzerainty treaty can be traced in miniature in the revelation written on the two tables by the finger of God.

"I am the Lord thy God," the opening words of the Sinaitic proclamation (Ex. 20:2a), correspond to the preamble of the zuzerainty treaties, which identified the zuzerain, or "great king," and that in terms calculated to inspire awe and fear. For example, the treaty of Mursilis with his vassal Duppi-Tessub of Amurru begins: "These are the words of the Sun Mursilis, the great king, the king of the Hatti land, the valiant, the favorite of the Storm-god, the son of Suppiluliumas, etc."[3]

Such treaties continued in an "I-thou" style with an historical prologue, surveying the great king's previous relations with, and especially his benefactions to, the vassal king. In the treaty just referred to, Mursilis reminds Duppi-Tessub of the vassal status of his father and grandfather, of their loyalty and enjoyment of Mursilis' just oversight, and climactically there is narrated how Mursilis, true to his promise to Duppi-Tessub's father, secured the dynastic succession for Duppi-Tessub, sick and ailing though he was. In the Decalogue, the historical prologue is found in the further words of the Lord: "which have brought thee out of the land of Egypt, out of the house of bondage" (Ex. 20:2b). This element in the covenant document was clearly designed to inspire confidence and gratitude in the vassal and thereby to dispose him to attend to the covenant obligations, which constitute the third element in both Exodus 20 and the international treaties.

There are many interesting parallels to specific biblical requirements among the treaty stipulations; but to mention only the most prominent, the fundamental demand is always for thorough commitment to the suzerain to the exclusion of all

3. Translation of A. Goetze in ed. James B. Pritchard: *Ancient Near Eastern Texts*, Princeton, 1950, p. 203. *Cf.* V. Korošeç, *Hethitische Staatsverträge*, Leipzig, 1931, pp. 36ff.

alien alliances.[4] Thus, Mursilis insists: "But you, Duppi-Tessub, remain loyal toward the king of the Hatti land, the Hatti land, my sons (and) my grandsons forever . . . . Do not turn your eyes to anyone else!"[5] And Yahweh commands his servant: "Thou shalt have no other gods before me" (Ex. 20:3; cf. vv. 4, 5).

Stylistically, the apodictic form of the Decalogue apparently finds its only parallel in the treaties, which contain categorical imperatives and prohibitions and a conditional type of formulation equivalent to the apodictic curse (cf. Deut. 27:15-26), both being directly oriented to covenant oaths and sanctions. The legislation in the extant legal codes, on the other hand, is uniformly of the casuistic type.

Two other standard features of the classic suzerainty treaty were the invocation of the gods of the suzerain and (in the Hittite sphere) the gods of the vassal as witnesses of the oath and the pronouncing of imprecations and benedictions, which the oath deities were to execute according to the vassal's deserts.

Obviously in the case of God's covenant with Israel there could be no thought of a realistic invocation of a third party as divine witness.[6] Indeed, it is implicit in the third word of the Decalogue that all Israel's oaths must be sworn by the name of Yahweh (Ex. 20:7). The immediate contextual application of this commandment is that the Israelite must remain true to the oath he was about to take at Sinai in accordance with the standard procedure in ceremonies of covenant ratification (cf. Ex. 24).

Mendenhall[7] finds no reference to an oath as the foundation of the Sinaitic covenant; he does, however, allow that the oath may have taken the form of a symbolic act rather than a verbal formula. But surely a solemn affirmation of consecration to God made in the presence of God to his mediator-representative and in response to divine demand, sanctioned by divine threats

---

4. Cf. further, Korošeç, *op. cit.*, pp. 66ff.; D. J. Wiseman, *The Vassal-Treaties of Esarhaddon*, London, 1958, pp. 23ff.; Mendenhall, *op. cit.*, p. 59.

5. *Ancient Near Eastern Texts*, p. 204.

6. There is a formal literary approximation to the invocation of the oath witnesses in Deut. 4:26; 30:19; and 31:28 where by the rhetorical device of apostrophe God calls heaven and earth to be witnesses of his covenant with Israel. Heaven and earth are also invoked along with the mountains and rivers, *etc.*, at the close of this section in the treaties. *Cf.* Matt. 5:34, 35; 23:16-22.

7. *Op. cit.*, p. 66.

against the rebellious, is tantamount to an oath. Moreover, Israel's eating and drinking in the persons of her representatives on the mount of God (Ex. 24:11) was a recognized symbolic method by which people swore treaties.[8]

The curses and blessings are present in Exodus 20, though not as a separate section. They are rather interspersed among the stipulations (see vv. 5, 6, 7, 11, and 12). Moreover, an adaptation of the customary form of the curses and blessings to the divine nature of the Suzerain who here pronounced them was necessary. Thus, the usual invocative form has yielded to the declarative, and that in the style of the motive clause, which is characteristic of Old Testament legislation and which is illustrative of what may be called the reasonableness of Israel's Lord.[9]

There is one final point of material correspondence between Exodus 20 and the secular treaties. It provides the key to the nature of the two tables of stone and to this we shall presently return. The parallelism already noted, however, is sufficient to demonstrate that the revelation committed to the two tables was rather a suzerainty treaty or covenant than a legal code. The customary exclusive use of "Decalogue" to designate this revelation, biblical terminology though it is (*cf.* "the ten words,"[10] Ex. 34:28; Deut. 4:13; 10:4), has unfortunately served to obscure the whole truth of the matter. That this designation is intended as only *pars pro toto* is confirmed by the fact that "covenant" (*berît;* Deut. 4:13) and "the words of the covenant" (Ex. 34:28) are alternate biblical terminology. So, too, is "testimony" ('ēdût; Ex. 25:16, 21; 40:20; *cf.* II Kgs. 17:15), which characterizes the stipulations as oath-bound obligations or as a covenant order of life.[11] Consequently, the two

8. *Cf.* Wiseman, *op. cit.,* p. 84 and lines 154-156 of the Ramataia text.

9. *Cf.* B. Gemser, "The importance of the motive clause in Old Testament law," *Supplements to Vetus Testamentum,* I (1953), pp. 50-66. It must be borne in mind that the Decalogue does not stand alone as the total revelation of the covenant at Sinai. For curses and blessings see also the conclusion of the Book of the Covenant (Ex. 23:20-33) and especially Deuteronomy 27-30.

10. The contents of the treaties are also called the "words" of the suzerain.

11. 'ēdût is related to the Akkadian adē, which is used as a general appellation for the contents of suzerainty treaties. Wiseman (*op. cit.,* p. 81), defines adū (sing.) as "a law or commandment solemnly imposed in the presence of divine witnesses by a suzerain upon an individual or people who have no option but acceptance of the terms. It implies a 'solemn

tables are called "the tables of the covenant" (Deut. 9:9, 11, 15) and "the tables of the testimony" (Ex. 31:18; 32:15; 34:29); the ark, as the depository of the tables, "the ark of the covenant" or "of the testimony"; and the tabernacle, where the ark was located, "the tabernacle of the testimony."

The two stone tables are not, therefore, to be likened to a stele containing one of the half-dozen or so known legal codes earlier than or roughly contemporary with Moses as though God had engraved on these tables a corpus of law.[12] The revelation they contain is nothing less than an epitome of the covenant granted by Yahweh, the sovereign Lord of heaven and earth, to his elect and redeemed servant, Israel.

Not law, but covenant. That must be affirmed when we are seeking a category comprehensive enough to do justice to this revelation in its totality. At the same time, the prominence of the stipulations, reflected in the fact that "the ten words" are the element used as *pars pro toto*, signalizes the centrality of law in this type of covenant. There is probably no clearer direction afforded the biblical theologian for defining with biblical emphasis the type of covenant God adopted to formalize his relationship to his people than that given in the covenant he gave Israel to perform, even "the ten commandments." Such a covenant is a declaration of God's lordship, consecrating a people to himself in a sovereignly dictated order of life.

But what now is the significance of the fact that the covenant was recorded not on one but on two stone tables?

Apart from the dubious symbolic propriety of bisecting a treaty for distribution over two separate documents, all the

charge or undertaking on oath' (according to the view of the suzerain or vassal) ."

12. There does appear to be some literary relationship between the legal codes and the suzerainty treaties. J. Muilenburg ("The form and structure of the covenantal formulations," *Vetus Testamentum*, IX (Oct. 1959) 4, pp. 347ff.) classifies both under "the royal message." Hammurapi in his code, which is still the most complete of the extant ancient Oriental codes, introduces himself in the prologue with a recital of his incomparable qualifications for the promulgation of laws, then presents the laws, and in the epilogue pronounces curses and blessings on future kings as they ignore or honor his code. The identity of the Decalogue with the suzerainty treaties over against such law codes is evidenced by features like the covenant terminology, the *adē* character of the stipulations, the "I-thou" formulation, and the purpose of the whole as manifested both in the contents and the historical occasion, *i.e.*, the establishment of a covenant relationship between two parties.

traditional suggestions as to how the division should be made are liable to the objection that they do violence to the formal and logical structure of this treaty. The results of the traditional type of cleavage are not two reasonably balanced sets of laws but one table containing almost all of three of the four treaty elements plus a part of the fourth, *i.e.*, the stipulations, and a second table with only a fraction of the stipulations and possibly a blessing formula. The preamble and historical prologue must be neither minimized nor ignored because of their brevity for this is a covenant in miniature. In comparison with the full-scale version, the stipulations are proportionately as greatly reduced as are the preamble and the historical prologue. That would be even clearer if the additional strand of the curses and blessings were not interwoven with the commandments. Certainly, too, there was no physical necessity for distributing the material over two stones. One table of such a size that Moses could carry, and the ark contain, a pair of them would offer no problem of spatial limitations to prevent engraving the entire text upon it, especially since the writing covered both obverse and reverse (Ex. 32:15). In fact, it seems unreasonable, judging from the appearance of comparable stone inscriptions from antiquity, to suppose that all the area on both sides of two tables would be devoted to so few words.

There is, moreover, the comparative evidence of the extrabiblical treaties. Covenants, such as Exodus 20:2-17 has been shown to be, are found written in their entirety on one table and indeed, like the Sinaitic tables, on both its sides.[13] As a further detail in the parallelism of external appearance it is tempting to see in the sabbath sign presented in the midst of the ten words the equivalent of the suzerain's dynastic seal found in the midst of the obverse of the international treaty documents.[14] Since in the case of the Decalogue the suzerain is Yahweh, there will be no representation of him on his seal, but the sabbath is declared to be his "sign of the covenant" (Ex. 31:13-17). By means of his sabbath-keeping, the image-

---

13. *Cf.*, *e.g.*, Wiseman, *op. cit.*, plates I and IX.

14. The closing paragraph of the Egyptian text of the parity treaty of Hattusilis III and Ramses II is a description of the seal, called "What is in the middle of the tablet of silver" (*Ancient Near Eastern Texts*, p. 201). For the Mitannian practice of placing the seal on the reverse, *cf.* D. J. Wiseman, *The Alalakh Tablets*, London, 1953, plates VII and VIII, texts 13 and 14.

bearer of God images the pattern of that divine act of creation which proclaims God's absolute sovereignty over man, and thereby he pledges his covenant consecration to his Maker. The Creator has stamped on world history the sign of the sabbath as his seal of ownership and authority. That is precisely what the pictures on the dynastic seals symbolize and their captions claim in behalf of the treaty gods and their representative, the suzerain.

These considerations point to the conclusion that each stone table was complete in itself. The two tables were duplicate copies of the covenant. And the correctness of this interpretation is decisively confirmed by the fact that it was normal procedure in establishing suzerainty covenants to prepare duplicate copies of the treaty text.

Five of the six standard sections of the classic suzerainty treaty were mentioned above. The sixth section contained directions for the depositing of one copy of the treaty document in a sanctuary of the vassal and another in a sanctuary of the suzerain.[15] For example, the treaty made by Suppiluliuma with Mattiwaza states: "A duplicate of this tablet has been deposited before the Sun-goddess of Arinna . . . . In the Mitanni land (a duplicate) has been deposited before Tessub . . . . At regular *intervals* shall they read it in the presence of the king of the Mitanni land and in the presence of the sons of the Hurri country."[16] Enshrinement of the treaty before the gods was expressive of their role as witnesses and avengers of the oath. Even the vassal's gods were thereby enlisted in the foreign service of the suzerain.[17]

Similar instructions were given Moses at Sinai concerning the two tables. They were to be deposited in the ark, which in turn was to be placed in the tabernacle (Ex. 25:16, 21; 40:20; Deut. 10:2). Because Yahweh was at once Israel's covenant Suzerain and God of Israel and Israel's oath, there was but one sanctuary for the depositing of both treaty duplicates. The spec-

---

15. *Cf.* Korošeç, *op. cit.*, pp. 100-101. On a stele from Ras Shamra an oath-taking ceremony is depicted with the two parties raising their hands over two copies of the treaty (*Ugaritica* III, plate VI).

16. Translation of A. Goetze, *Ancient Near Eastern Texts*, p. 205. In various treaties the public reading requirement specifies from once to thrice annually.

17. *Cf.* II Kgs. 18:25 and observations of M. Tsevat, "The Neo-Assyrian and Neo-Babylonian Vassal Oaths and the Prophet Ezekiel," *Journal of Biblical Literature*, LXXVIII (Sept. 1959) III, p. 199.

ified location of the documents as given in Hittite treaties can be rendered "under (the feet of)" the god, which would then correspond strikingly to the arrangements in the Israelite holy of holies.[18] The two tables do not themselves contain instructions concerning their disposition, for the legislation regarding the ark and sanctuary had not yet been given. The same is true of the Book of the Covenant (Ex. 20:22-23:33). But it is significant that when such legislation was given after the ceremony of covenant ratification (Ex. 24), the ark was the first object described in detail and directions for depositing the two tables in it were included (Ex. 25:10-22).

As for the further custom of periodic public reading of treaty documents, the contents of the two tables were of course declared in the hearing of all Israel and the Book of the Covenant was read to the people as part of the ratification ceremony (Ex. 24:7); but the practice of periodic proclamation was first formulated some forty years later in the Book of Deuteronomy when God was renewing the covenant unto the second generation. When suzerainty covenants were renewed, new documents were prepared in which the stipulations were brought up to date. Deuteronomy is such a covenant renewal document; hence its repetition with modernizing modifications of the earlier legislation, as found, for example, in its treatment of the Decalogue (5:6-21) or of the Passover (16:5ff.; cf. Ex. 12:7, 46).[19] Another case in point is Deuteronomy's addition of this requirement for the regular public reading of the covenant law at the feast of Tabernacles in the seventh year of release (31:9-13), a requirement that became relevant and applicable with the arrival of the Israelites at the threshold of their inheritance in Canaan. The document which was to be brought forth and read was not one of the stone tables but the "book of the law" which Moses wrote and had placed by the side of the ark (31:9, 26). However, even if "this book of the law" is identified with Deuteronomy alone, reading it would have included a re-proclamation of the contents of the tables.

18. See Ex. 25:22. Cf. Korošeç op. cit., p. 100.
19. Taking Pentateuchal history at its face value, we discover that the Book of Deuteronomy exhibits precisely the legal form which contemporary second millennium B.C. evidence indicates a suzerain would employ in his rule of a vassal nation like Israel at such an historical juncture. See further Chapter 2.

The relevance of the foregoing for higher critical conclusions concerning the Decalogue may be noted in passing. Along with a decreasing reluctance in negative critical studies to accept the Mosaic origin of the Decalogue,[20] the judgment continues that the present form of the Sinaitic Decalogue is an expansion of the original, which is then reduced to an abridged version of the ten words, without preamble, historical prologue, or curses and blessings, and often without even an abridged form of the second and fourth words. Similarly, even where there is no bias against the Bible's representations concerning its own origins, the supposition has gained currency that it was an abbreviated version of the Decalogue that was engraved on the stone tables. Such estimates of the contents of the Mosaic tables are clearly unsatisfactory, since the supposed abbreviated forms lack those very features which distinguish the tables as that which comparative study indicates was called for by the historical occasion, and biblical exegesis indicates the tables to be, not a brief ethical catechism, but copies of the Sinaitic covenant.

The purpose of Israel's copy of the covenant was that of a documentary witness (Deut. 31:26).[21] It was witness to and against Israel, reminding of obligations sworn to and rebuking for obligations violated, declaring the hope of covenant beatitude and pronouncing the doom of the covenant curses. The public proclamation of it was designed to teach the fear of the Lord to all Israel, especially to the children (Deut. 31:13; cf. Ps. 78:5ff.).

The secular treaties and the biblical covenant share a perspective of family solidarity reflected in numerous references to the sons and grandsons of the vassal. In the political treaties, sworn commitment is in the terms: "we, our sons, and our grandsons"; and agreeably both curses and blessings are pronounced unto children's children. "Visiting the iniquity of the fathers upon the children unto the third and fourth generation of them that hate me" (Ex. 20:5b) is the biblical counterpart, defining the bounds of corporate responsibility in guilt under

20. Cf. H. H. Rowley, "Moses and the Decalogue," *Bulletin of the John Rylands Library*, xxxiv, 1951-52, pp. 81ff.
21. Various types of covenant witnesses other than the divine witness are mentioned. Cf. the Song of Moses, which he had Israel memorize (Deut. 31:19, 22; 32:1ff.); the stones with the law written upon them erected on Ebal (Deut. 27:2ff.; Josh. 8:30-35); and the stone witness of covenant renewal at Shechem (Josh. 24:26, 27).

this covenant administration by the utmost limits of contemporaneity (here described by means of numerical climax, a popular device of Hebrew and Canaanite literature).

Both copies of the covenant were laid before Yahweh as God of the oath. But what was the purpose of Yahweh's own copy in his capacity as covenant Suzerain? In the case of the international treaties, the suzerain would naturally want to possess, preserve, and protect a sealed legal witness to the treaty. It would remind him of the vassal's *adē* for the purpose of enforcement and punishment; for he would be the actual avenger of the oath, the instrument of the oath deities according to the religious theory which was the legal fiction lending sacred sanction to the treaty. It would also remind him of his suzerain's role as protector of the vassal and of the various specific promises of assistance often contained in the treaties. He had not, however, like the vassal, taken a covenant oath and human lords being what they are he would have considerably less interest in the benefits he might bestow than in the amount of annual tribute he was entitled to exact from the vassal.

Such *mutatis mutandis* was the purpose of Yahweh's own stone table of covenant witness. However, even from the formal point of view there is here a remarkable shift in emphasis arising from the fact that God's suzerainty covenant with Israel was an administration of salvation. The form of the blessing suggests the unique emphasis: "showing mercy," and that not merely to the third and fourth generation of them that love him but, contrary to the balance observed in this respect in the curse and blessing formulae of the international treaties, "to a thousand generations" (Deut. 7:9). This much more abounding of grace is evidenced even in connection with the function of the stone tables as witnesses against Israel; for since the divine throne under which the tables were located was the place of atonement, the witness of the tables against Israel never ascended to Yahweh apart from the witness of the blood advocating mercy.

The divine Suzerain's condescension in his redemptive covenant at the time of its Abrahamic administration extended to the humiliation of swearing himself to covenant fidelity as Lord of the covenant and Fulfiller of the promises (Gen. 15). Mendenhall[22] mistakenly regards the Abrahamic Covenant as com-

22. *Op. cit.*, p. 62.

pletely different in kind from the Sinaitic, partly because of God's oath and partly because of an alleged absence of obligations imposed on Abraham. Actually, the total allegiance to his Lord demanded of Abraham (see Gen. 12:1; 17:1) was precisely that fealty which the treaty stipulations were designed to secure.

Moreover, it is demonstrable that an oath on the part of the suzerain was not incompatible with the genius of the relationship governed by a suzerainty treaty. There are, for example, a treaty and a related deed from Alalakh,[23] both concerned with one Abban, the vizier of Hattusa, and his bestowment of certain cities upon his political "servant" Iarimlim. The treaty states that Abban confirmed the gift in perpetuity by a self-maledictory oath accompanied by the symbolism of slaughtering a sheep. It also stipulates that the territorial gift is forfeit if Iarimlim is disloyal to Abban. The text deeding Alalakh (part of Abban's gift) pronounces curses upon any who would alter Abban's purpose by hostilities against Iarimlim. All this corresponds perfectly to God's dealings with Abraham. The Lord covenanted territory to his servant Abraham as an everlasting possession (Gen. 12:1, 2; 13:14-17; 15:18) and did so by a self-maledictory oath symbolized by the slaying of animals (Gen. 15:9ff.). Moreover, it is clear that by rebellion against Yahweh's word Abraham would forfeit the promise (Gen. 22:16, 17a; cf. Deut. 28, especially vv. 63ff.); and finally, the Egyptians and Canaanites who would oppose this territorial grant were cursed (Gen. 12:3; 15:14, 16, 19-21).

God's oath is, therefore, in keeping with the suzerain-vassal relationship. The generic nature of God's covenants with his people remains first and last a declaration of divine lordship, a lordship which may be manifested in the execution of promises or threats. These covenants are sovereign administrations not of blessing exclusively but of curse and blessing according to the vassal's deserts. Since, however, the specifically soteric covenants are informed by the principle of God's sovereign grace, which infallibly effects his redemptive purposes in Christ, they are accompanied by divine guarantees assuring a realization of the blessing sanctions of the covenant. Now it

23. Published by D. J. Wiseman in the *Journal of Cuneiform Studies* XII (Dec. 1958) 4, pp. 124-129 and in *The Alalakh Tablets* (London, 1953), pp. 25, 26, plate I, respectively.

would obviously be unsound methodology to give this special feature which belongs to the specifically redemptive covenant administrations a constitutive place when defining the covenant generically. Nevertheless, divine guarantees of blessing such as God's oath to Abraham, guarantees which, without violating human responsibility, assure to the elect vassals that in Christ they will receive that covenant righteousness which is the stipulated way to covenant beatitude, such guarantees are not in the least incompatible with the nature of suzerainty covenants as here defined in terms of divine lordship, enforced in a revelation of law consisting of stipulations and sanctions, both promissory and penal.

Considered in relation to the divine oath and promise, Yahweh's duplicate table of the covenant served a purpose analogous to that of the rainbow in his covenant with Noah (Gen. 9:13-16). Beholding this table, he remembered his oath to his servants and faithfully brought to pass the promised blessing. And in that day when the four and twenty heavenly elders worship him saying, "Thy wrath is come, and the time of the dead, that they should be judged, and that thou shouldest give reward unto thy servants the prophets, and to the saints, and them that fear thy name, small and great," then appropriately, the temple of God in heaven being opened, there is seen in his temple the ark of his covenant, the depository of God's table of remembrance (Rev. 11:17-19).

There remains the question of the relevance of our interpretation of the duplicate tables of the covenant for the understanding of their law content. The increased emphasis on the covenantal context of the law underscores the essential continuity in the function of law in the Old and New Testaments. The Decalogue is not offered fallen man as a genuine soteric option but is presented as a guide to citizenship within the covenant by the Saviour-Lord, who of his mercy delivers out of the house of bondage into communion in the life of the covenant — a communion which eventuates in perfect conformity of life to the law of the covenant. To stress the covenantal "I-thou" nature of this law is also to reaffirm the personal-religious character of biblical ethics at the same time that it recognizes that covenantal religion and its ethics are susceptible of communication in the form of structured truth. Yahweh describes the beneficiaries of his mercy as "them that love me and keep my commandments" (Ex. 20:6; *cf.* John 14:15).

Recognition of the completeness of each of the tables provides a corrective to the traditional view's obscuration of the covenantal-religious nature of the laws in "the second table." A hegemony of religion over ethics has, indeed, always been predicated on the basis of the priority in order and verbal quantity of the laws of "the first table," analyzed as duty or love to God, over the laws of "the second table," analyzed as duty or love to man. Nevertheless, this very division of the ten words into "two tables" with the category "love of God" used as a means of separating one "table" from the other is liable to the misunderstanding that the fulfillment of the demands of "the second table" is to some degree, if not wholly, independent of the principle of love for God.

Our Lord's familiar teaching concerning a "first and great commandment" and a "second like unto it" (Matt. 22:37-40; Mark 12:29-31) has figured prominently in the speculation about the contents of "the two tables."[24] It is, however, gratuitous to suppose that Jesus was epitomizing in turn a "first table" and "second table" as traditionally conceived.[25] Furthermore, it must be seriously questioned whether Jesus' commandment to love God's image-bearer, ourselves and our neighbors alike, can properly be restricted after the dominant fashion to the fifth through the tenth laws. The nearest parallel in the Decalogue to the specific language of Jesus is found in the fourth law as formulated in Deuteronomy (5:14): The sabbath is to be kept "that thy manservant and thy maidservant may rest as well as thou." And does man not best serve the eternal interests of himself and his neighbor when he promotes obedience to the first three commandments? Is that not the ethical justification of the great commission?

But beyond all doubt Jesus' "great commandment" must be the heart motive of man in the whole compass of his life. Restricting the principle of love of God to the sphere of worship would prejudice the comprehensiveness of God's absolute lordship which is the foundation of the covenant order.

24. In the Westminster Confession of Faith, for example, it is the only proof text cited for distinguishing between the "tables" in terms of duty towards God and duty to man (chap. XIX, sec. II).

25. There is no explicit reference to the two stone tables in the context, which is broadly concerned with the generality of scriptural legislation. Jesus relates his two commandments to the totality of Old Testament revelation (Matt. 22:40).

That the love of God with heart, soul, mind, and strength is as relevant to the tenth commandment as it is to the first is evident from the fact that to violate the tenth is to worship Mammon, and we cannot love and serve God and Mammon. Or consider the tenth word from the viewpoint of the principle of stewardship, the corollary of the principle of God's covenant lordship. Property in the Israelite theocracy was held only in fief under the Lord who declared: "For the land is mine; for ye are strangers and sojourners with me" (Lev. 25:23b). Therefore to covet the inheritance of one's neighbor was to covet what was God's[26] and so betray want of love for him. The application of this is universal because not just Canaan but "the earth is the Lord's and the fulness thereof, the world and they that dwell therein" (Ps. 24:1).

The comprehensiveness of Jesus' "first and great commandment" is evident from the preamble and historical prologue of the covenant document. Being introductory to the whole body of stipulations which follow, they are manifestly intended to inculcate the proper motivation for obedience not to three or four or five of the stipulations but to them all; and the motivation they inspire is that of love to the divine Redeemer. Why are we to love our neighbors? Because we love the God who loves them and, according to the principle articulated in the sabbath commandment (Ex. 20:11), the imperative to love God is also a demand to be like him.

The two commandments of Jesus do not distinguish two separable areas of human life but two complementary aspects of human responsibility. Our Lord's perspective is one with that of the duplicate tables of the covenant which comprehend the whole duty of man within the unity of his consecration to his covenant Lord.

---

26. Considered in this light, there is an exact equivalent to the tenth commandment in a Hittite treaty where the suzerain charges the vassal: "Thou shalt not desire any territory of the land of Hatti." (Cited by Mendenhall, "Ancient Oriental and Biblical Law," *The Biblical Archaeologist* XVII (May, 1954) 2, p. 30).

2. Dynastic Covenant

New winds are blowing on the bark of Deuteronomic studies. It has managed not to drift very far from its Josianic (7th century B.C.) dock only because of the unusually stout cables of critical traditionalism which tie it there.[1] The fate of so much higher critical treasure rides with this vessel that the scholarly merchants have been understandably anxious about its moorings and timid about entrusting it to the gods of wind and wave — especially since the winds appear to be blowing in the general direction of the Mosaic port, whence (so some say) the merchants pirated the craft.

Over twenty years ago Gerhard von Rad signalized the need for discovering the nature and meaning of the over-all form of Deuteronomy.[2] Attention had been paid to the individual *Gattung*, whether parenesis, legal precept, or curse and blessing formula. But what was the structural coherence of the several parts within the whole? In current discussions this question is of crucial significance because the problem of the unity of Deuteronomy is judged to be not stylistic but structural.[3] Higher criticism has sought to distinguish an original core of Deuteronomy from the alleged accretions. Wellhausen and others have limited this core to chapters 12-26 but due to the stylistic homogeneity most would now expand this to chapters 5-26 and 28. It is the remaining chapters which are thought to disturb the structural unity and are regarded as editorial appendages. A. C. Welch, who distinguishes a Deuteronomic code (beginning in chapter 12) and framework, finds confusion throughout, but deems the framework in particular so hopelessly disordered that he declares it misleading to speak of editing since

1. For a survey of the more recent recommendations for a pre-Josianic or post-Josianic dating see C. R. North, "Pentateuchal Criticism" in *The Old Testament and Modern Study* (ed. H. H. Rowley), Oxford, 1951, esp. pp. 49ff.

2. "Das formgeschichtliche Problem des Hexateuch," *Beiträge zur Wissenschaft vom Alten und Neuen Testament*, 4. Folge, Heft 26, 1938; reprinted in G. v. Rad, *Gesammelte Studien zum Alten Testament*, Munich, 1958.

3. *Cf.* G. E. Wright, Introduction to commentary on Deuteronomy in *The Interpreter's Bible*, Vol. 2, New York-Nashville, 1953, pp. 314-318.

that would suggest that a degree of order had been introduced into the chaos![4]

It is then with this issue of the structural unity and integrity of Deuteronomy that the present investigation is concerned. The question resolves itself into one of literary genre and *Sitz im Leben*. We believe it can be shown that what Mendenhall tentatively suggested concerning biblical history and law in general is certainly true in the case of Deuteronomy: ". . . the literary criticism of the past has been proceeding with completely inadequate form-critical presuppositions."[5] The position to be advocated here is that Deuteronomy is a covenant renewal document which in its total structure exhibits the classic legal form of the suzerainty treaties of the Mosaic age.[6] Our procedure will be to trace the parallelism from beginning to end, observing especially the integrity of those sections of Deuteronomy whose presence has posed problems for the unity of the book. In a brief article only major blocks of material can be considered but this will be sufficient to determine the validity of the thesis.

It will be useful to have a simple outline of the matter before us:[7] 1. Preamble (1:1-5). 2. Historical Prologue (1:6-4:49). 3. Stipulations (5-26). 4. Curses and Blessings or Covenant Ratification (27-30). 5. Succession Arrangements or Covenant Continuity, in which are included the invocation of witnesses and directions for the disposition and public reading of the treaty (31-34).

4. *Deuteronomy: The Framework to the Code,* Oxford, 1932, pp. 8ff.

5. "Covenant Forms in Israelite Tradition," *The Biblical Archaeologist,* XVII, 3 (Sept. 1954), p. 70, n. 45. *Cf.* C. H. Gordon's broad development of this theme in "New Horizons in Old Testament Literature," *Encounter* 21 (Spring, 1960) 2, pp. 131-160.

6. The present essay thus elaborates the identification of Deuteronomy made above; see Chapter One, note 19. While the pattern of the suzerainty treaty has been widely recognized in the Decalogue and in Joshua 24, there has been a strange lack of acknowledgment of all the obvious facts in the case of Deuteronomy. Unfortunately too, the covenant described in Joshua 24 has been interpreted on the horizontal level of a confederation of the twelve tribes with one another in an amphictyonic alliance rather than vertically as a renewal of Yahweh's lordship over the long since established theocracy. The very parallelism of the Joshua 24 covenant with the secular suzerainty treaties, as well as its clear continuity with and its obvious presupposing of the earlier Mosaic covenants, contradicts the interpretation of this event as the founding of the twelve tribe system in Israel.

7. For a descriptive account of the treaty pattern see above, pp. 14ff.

To analyze Deuteronomy in terms of a documentary pattern is not incompatible with the obvious fact that the book according to its own representations consists almost entirely of a series of addresses. For the specific kind of document in view would be orally proclaimed to the vassals at the covenant ceremony. Stylistically, this is reflected in the characteristic "I-thou" form of the suzerainty treaties, which is itself a point of correspondence with Deuteronomy. Also indicative of the oral proclamation of the covenant text is the evidence for the act of response by the vassal during the covenant ritual. Such a response is, in fact, incorporated into the very text of Esarhaddon's Nimrud treaty where it consists of a self-maledictory oath binding the vassal to the lord's stipulations, which are repeated in summary in the response.[8] Deuteronomy also mentions the Amen to be uttered by the Israelites in the course of their ceremony (Deut. 27:15-26; cf. 26:17, 18; 29:12; Ex. 24:7; Josh. 24:16-18, 21, 24).[9] The treaty document was thus the libretto of the covenant ceremony, sometimes including the response of the vassal as well as the declarations of the suzerain. When, therefore, we identify Deuteronomy as a treaty text we are also recognizing it as the ceremonial words of Moses. The customary conception of these Mosaic addresses as a freely ordered farewell must be so far modified as to recognize that their formal structure closely followed fixed ceremonial-legal traditions, though they are certainly no stereotyped liturgical recital nor the dispassionate product of an imperial foreign office.

It will be recognized that this approach has a degree of formal affinity with the views of von Rad. Noting the succession of parenesis based on historical recital (1-11), laws (12-26:15), covenant engagement (26:16-19), and blessings and curses (27ff.) — a combination found also in the Sinai pericope in Exodus 19-24 — von Rad concluded that this pattern points to the course of a great cultic celebration, specifically, an ancient covenant renewal festival at Shechem.[10] We have no sympathy for von Rad's failure to recognize the historicity of the covenant renewal

8. Lines 494-512; cf. D. J. Wiseman, *The Vassal-Treaties of Esarhaddon*, p. 26.

9. Similar is the Hittite soldiers' Amen to the curses spoken and symbolized when they were pledging their loyalty to the king of Hatti land. See *Ancient Near Eastern Texts* (hereafter, *A.N.E.T.*), pp. 353f.

10. *Cf. op. cit.* and *Studies in Deuteronomy*, London, 1953, pp. 14f. (translation of *Deuteronomium-Studien*, Göttingen, 1948).

presented in Deuteronomy as a particular ceremony conducted by Moses in Moab. Neither are we persuaded that there was a periodic cultic ceremony held at Shechem. However, von Rad's formal analysis of the literary structure of Deuteronomy, based on his association of it with an alleged covenant renewal ceremony, did approximate to what we judge to be the truth of the matter as that is now illuminated by the more recent studies of the international treaties. In their light the answer to the problem of Deuteronomy's literary genre can be formulated more accurately and fully than was possible in von Rad's studies.

Deuteronomy begins precisely as the ancient treaties began: "These are the words of . . . ."[11] The Jewish custom of using the opening words of a book as its title turns out in the present case to be most felicitous for it serves to identify this book at once as a treaty document.[12] Deuteronomy 1:1-5 then goes on to identify the speaker of "the words" as Moses, one who receives divine revelation and communicates the sovereign will of the Lord to Israel. Yahweh is, therefore, the Suzerain who gives the covenant and Moses is his vicegerent and the covenant mediator. This section thus corresponds to the preamble of the extra-biblical treaties, which also identified the speaker, the one who by the covenant was declaring his lordship and claiming the vassal's allegiance.[13]

"A major problem concerning the unity of Deuteronomy has been the presence of the two introductions (chs. 1-4 and 5-11) to the legal section in chs. 12-26. Neither introduction needs the other; they seem to be independent of each other." So states G. E. Wright,[14] and then adopts M. Noth's solution. This solution is bound up with the larger issue of Deuteronomy's relation to other canonical books. Noth,[15] like Engnell, would detach Deuteronomy from the Pentateuch and attach it to the Former Prophets thus making it the beginning of and philosophy for a Deuteronomic history continuing through II Kings. The opening chapters of Deuteronomy are, according to Noth, an

11. Wherever the beginning of the Hittite suzerainty treaties is preserved, *umma*, the particle used for introducing direct discourse, is found. Compare, too, the Bible's familiar introductory formula: "Thus saith the Lord."

12. Altogether misleading, on the contrary, is the English title, which is apparently based on the Septuagint's mistranslation of the phrase, "a copy of this law" (17:18) as *to deuteronomion touto*, "this second law."

13. *Cf.* above, p. 14.

14. *Op. cit.*, p. 316, n. 13.

15. *Ueberlieferungsgeschichtliche Studien* I, Halle, 1943.

introduction to this history as a whole and that leaves the Deuteronomic laws as such with only one introduction, i.e., chapters 5 (or 4:44) -11.

But Noth's view (and every attempt to separate Deuteronomy 1-4 from an original core) is contradicted, the supposed problem of the two introductions is obviated, and the real structure of Deuteronomy is further clarified by these facts: an historical prologue regularly follows the preamble and precedes the stipulations in the suzerainty treaties[16] and Deuteronomy 1:5-4:49 qualifies admirably as such an historical prologue.[17] When covenants were renewed the history was brought up to date. Agreeably, Moses takes up the narrative of Yahweh's previous rule over Israel at Horeb where the theocratic covenant was originally made (though Moses, as often elsewhere, roots the development in the earlier Abrahamic Covenant, 1:8) and he carries the history to the present, emphasizing the most recent events, the Transjordanian conquests and their consequences.

Deuteronomy 4 is noteworthy in that it exhibits to a degree at least each of the constitutive features of the treaty pattern: the identification of the speaker (vv. 1, 2, 5, 10), the appeal to covenant history (vv. 10ff., 20ff., etc.), the basic stipulation of undivided allegiance (vv. 15ff., etc.), the blessing-curse sanctions (vv. 27ff.), the invocation of witnesses (v. 26), and the arrangements for the perpetuation of the covenant (vv. 9, 10, 21, 22). This reflection of the total treaty pattern within the undisputed unity of this brief passage is a significant clue to the nature of the larger document in which it is embedded and an interesting indication of how Moses' thought and expression this day were operating within the traditional forms required by the occasion. In his mind he sees the whole course of the ceremony with its call for decision and solemn sanctions and in the urgency of these his final words to the people whom he has so long served he summarily anticipates all that is about to transpire.

The third division of suzerainty treaties was the stipulations,[18] and this division in Deuteronomy can be readily identified with chapters 5-26. Von Rad, as noted above, included chapters

---

16. Cf. above, p. 14.
17. Deut. 4:44-49 may be assigned to the historical prologue or to the following stipulations; it provides a summarizing conclusion for the one and introduction to the other and is thus transitional.
18. Cf. above, pp. 14ff.

5-11 with 1-4 as a parenetic historical survey. Others, separating chapters 5-11 from 1-4, regard them as an introduction to chapters 12-26. But Deuteronomy 5-11 must be recognized as expounding the covenant way of life just as do chapters 12-26. Together they declare the Suzerain's demands. The differences between Deuteronomy 5-11 and 12-26 only represent differing treatments of this one theme. The former section presents in more general and comprehensive terms the primary demand for consecration to the Lord, both as principle (6) and program (7); the latter adds the more specific, ancillary requirements. Of particular interest is the fact that this sequence from the fundamental to the auxiliary commandments corresponds to the arrangement of the stipulations observable in the extra-biblical treaties. They first formulate the basic demand for tributary allegiance, then proceed to the details of military cooperation, extradition, etc.[19]

One cannot but notice also how the programmatic mandate of conquest (Deut. 7), which implements the call for perfect loyalty to Yahweh by its demand for the obliteration of rival gods with their cults and devotees within Yahweh's chosen holy domain, corresponds to the military clauses in the treaties. Another interesting parallel is found in the Deuteronomic version of the customary stipulation forbidding the vassal to pay tribute to any but the covenant suzerain. This is noteworthy in connection with a denial of the integrity of Deuteronomy 12:1-7 like that of Welch. For it is this authentic treaty motif which clearly provides the rationale of the re-formulation of the earlier law of the central altar in Deuteronomy 12 and constitutes the underlying unity of all the precepts, permissions, and prohibitions in that chapter.

The hortatory character of the Deuteronomic stipulations, even of those in chapters 12-26, exposes the inaccuracy of speaking of a Deuteronomic law code. But this feature is not without parallel in the formulation of the treaty stipulations. We are reminded of Moses' recalling the lessons of Israel's past history when Mursilis enforces his demand for three hundred shekels of gold by exhorting Duppi-Tessub: "Do not turn your eyes to anyone else! Your fathers presented tribute to Egypt;

19. See the treaty between Mursilis and Duppi-Tessub in *A.N.E.T.*, pp. 203, 204, where the primary stipulation is separately paragraphed as "Future Relations of the Two Countries." A similar sequence is found in parity treaties; *cf. ibid.*, pp. 199-203.

you [shall not do that!]."[20] This documentary feature would naturally be fully exploited by Moses in conducting the renewal ceremony which was also his personal farewell and as impressive an occasion as ever challenged an orator. It is, therefore, a quite unnecessary and misguided effort when von Rad seeks to account for the interspersion of the commandments with parenesis in terms of later Levitical preaching of the law at a cultic festival.[21]

One further point of correspondence to the treaties may be mentioned in connection with the stipulations. Deuteronomy's repetition of the Decalogue and other earlier legislation, with such modifications as were required by Israel's imminent change of environment from desert to city and town, accords with the suzerains' practice of repeating but modernizing their demands when renewing covenants.[22]

In the covenant ceremony the vassal took his oath in response to the stipulations and under the sanctions of the curses and blessings, which are found as a fourth standard section in the treaties.[23] This decisive act in Israel's ceremony in Moab is reflected at the conclusion of the Deuteronomic stipulations (26:17-19; cf. Ex. 24:7) and within chapters 27-30 (especially 29:10-15; cf. 27:15-26), the Deuteronomic curse-blessing section. This element of promissory and penal sanctions which chapters 27-30 have in common, finding as it does its counterpart in content, context, and function in the extra-biblical covenant documents, evidences the unity of these chapters and their integrity within the total original Deuteronomic document. The usual scholarly conclusion that chapter 28 belongs with chapters 12-26 while chapters 27, 29, and 30 are unoriginal appendixes of unknown but late date betrays a lack of appreciation for the relevant form-critical data.[24] The fact that the curse-blessing motif in Deuteronomy 27 takes the form of directions for a subsequent ceremony to be conducted by Joshua at Shechem has lent itself to the dissociation of this chapter from its context.

20. Translation of A. Goetze, A.N.E.T., p. 204.
21. Cf. Studies in Deuteronomy, pp. 13ff.
22. Cf. above, p. 20.
23. Cf. above, pp. 15f.
24. Cf. G. E. Wright's remark: "Again the difficulty is largely structural" (op. cit., p. 317). Naturalistic stumbling over the preview of Israel's distant exile and restoration contained in these chapters has certainly contributed more to the dominant higher critical dating of them than have the alleged structural difficulties.

But, as will be shown below, if Deuteronomy's own account of its historical origins is respected and the significance of the theme of dynastic succession is properly appraised, the integrity of Deuteronomy 27 becomes apparent.

In this section as in Deuteronomy 4 an accumulation of the major treaty elements is discovered within short compass, forming a concentrated covenant pattern as the framework for the great call for decision (30:15-20). There is historical recital of the Lord's mighty acts of grace (29:2ff.); a reiteration of the primary stipulation to love God, with the corollary prohibition of alien alliances (29:18ff.); the invocation of heaven and earth as witnesses (30:19); and, of course, the curses and blessings throughout chapters 27-30.

Worthy of parenthetical comment is the fact that the Mosaic curses and blessings provided the outline for the eschatological message of the prophets. In the nature of the case the blessings and curses of a covenant whose lord was Yahweh, sovereign Judge of history, could not but be prophecy. If it had been recognized earlier that the common roots of prophetic woe and weal are located here in the sanctions of Israel's ancient covenant, the tendency of literary criticism to distinguish sharply between the provenance of the weal and woe strands in the deliverances of the prophets might have been forestalled. Awareness of this unity of the antonymic sanctions within the *literary* tradition of covenant documents should also serve to dampen the more recent enthusiasm for tracing the judgment-restoration theme of the prophets to a hypothetical Israelite cultic drama of disaster and deliverance.[25]

The closing chapters (31-34) have been generally dismissed as miscellaneous appendixes. If, however, one looks beyond the surface fact that there is a variety of literary forms in these chapters and takes his analytical cue from the treaty pattern observable in the book hitherto, he is bound to come to quite another conclusion. For Deuteronomy 31-34 is consistently concerned with the continuity and perpetuation of the covenant relationship and all the elements in this section serve to corroborate the identification of Deuteronomy in its entirety as a unified suzerainty treaty.

---

25. *Cf.* F. Charles Fensham, "Malediction and Benediction in Ancient Near Eastern Vassal-Treaties and the Old Testament," *Zeitschrift für die Alttestamentliche Wissenschaft* 74 (1962) 1, pp. 1-9.

Included here are the final two standard elements in the classic treaty structure. One is the enlisting of witnesses to the covenant. Heaven and earth are again summoned to this office (31:28; 32:1; cf. 4:26; 30:19) but most prominent is the Song of Witness (31:16-22; 31:28-32:45), which is to be in Israel's own mouth as God's witness against them in the days to come (31:19).[26] The other customary feature is the direction for the depositing of the treaty text in the sanctuary and its periodic reproclamation (31:9-13).[27] This arrangement, while it served the end of perpetuating the covenant in that it was a means for the inspirational instruction of successive generations in the words of God's law (31:12, 13; 32:46), was yet another witness to the covenant (31:26).

For the rest, the closing chapters are concerned in one way or another with the Moses-Joshua succession. This succession was appointive and charismatic, not genealogical, but in so far as these men were mediators between God and Israel and thus successive representatives of the unchanging rule of Yahweh over Israel, their succession may be designated dynastic. There was indeed a peculiar unity between Moses and Joshua. The earlier intimate association of Joshua with Moses in the latter's mediatorial prerogatives on the Sinaitic mount of theophany suggests a kind of identification — a "dynastic" oneness of the two. Moreover, the work accomplished through the two was one redemptive complex, the one great Old Testament salvation consisting in deliverance from Egypt and inheritance of Canaan. It was Moses' anticipation that he should complete this work himself, but unexpectedly he was disqualified and was obliged to ascend the mount to die. Joshua, however, might be thought of as a Moses *redivivus*. Continuing in the spirit and power of Moses he completes the soteric drama begun under Moses. Joshua perfects the typological unit: out of bondage into paradise land. It is, of course, only in terms of such human mediatorial representatives that dynastic succession is predicable of the rule of the King eternal, immortal, invisible; but at that level there does exist a theocratic analogy to dynastic succession in human kingdoms.

---

26. *Cf.* above, p. 15. On the literary form of the Song of Witness in Deut. 32 see the valuable article by Julien Harvey, "Le 'Rîb-Pattern', réquisitoire prophétique sur la rupture de l'alliance" in *Biblica*, 43 (1962) 2, pp. 172-196.

27. *Cf.* above, pp. 19f.

This subject of the royal succession clearly contributes to the motif of covenant continuity and hence enhances the thematic coherence of Deuteronomy 31-34. But it is also a further mark of Deuteronomy's literary identity. For the throne succession of the suzerain's house figures very prominently in the suzerainty treaties.[28] In fact, the vassal's oath of allegiance was directed to both the suzerain and his successors. Most significant of the available evidence on this point is the Nimrud treaty of Esarhaddon, for it is occupied exclusively with this one subject of royal succession.[29] It is the text of the covenant ceremony at which Esarhaddon's vassals were required to acknowledge by oath the succession rights of Ashurbanipal as crown prince of Assyria and of his brother Shamash-shum-ukin as crown prince of Babylonia.[30]

In this connection there comes into focus the two-stage nature of Yahweh's ceremonial renewal of his covenant with Israel. The ceremony insuring Ashurbanipal's throne rights was held, as it turned out, just four years before the elderly Esarhaddon's death. Then, as was customary, soon after the accession of Ashurbanipal there was another ceremony for the confirming of the vassals' fealty to him.[31] Such, we take it, is the relationship of the covenant ceremony conducted by Moses in Moab and documented by the Book of Deuteronomy to the covenant ceremony conducted by Joshua at Mounts Ebal and Gerizim and reported in Joshua 8:30-35. The first stage takes place when the death of Moses, the Lord's representative, is imminent.[32] Yahweh's continuing lordship is reaffirmed in a ceremony in which his appointment of Joshua to be Moses' successor as his vicegerent is announced (31:3) and Joshua is

---

28. Cf. V. Korošeç, Hethitische Staatsverträge, pp. 66, 67; cf. pp. 63f.

29. See D. J. Wiseman, op. cit., esp. p. 28.

30. Legal provision is also made in the treaties with respect to the dynastic succession within the vassal kingdom. So, for example, Suppiluliuma stipulates that the Mitannian throne succession shall go to the offspring of the marriage of the vassal Mattiwaza and Suppiluliuma's daughter (cf. Korošeç, op. cit., p. 70). This concern with the vassal dynasty might also offer a counterpart to the Moses-Joshua succession in Deuteronomy, for the dual character of their mediatorial role meant that they were not only God's vicegerents over Israel but Israel's representatives before God and thus a charismatic "dynasty" of vassal kings.

31. See Wiseman's introductory study, op. cit.

32. If Moses and Joshua were being viewed as vassal kings, the timing of the covenant renewal could be related to the practice of renewing suzerainty treaties when death occasioned a change of vassal rulers.

divinely commissioned (31:14, 23; cf. 31:7ff.). Accordingly Israel's renewed oath of obedience to the Lord embraces a commitment to follow Joshua (cf. 34:9; Josh. 1:16-18), that is, to submit to Yahweh's expressed will regarding the dynastic succession. The second stage of the ceremony was held at Shechem not long after Moses' death and Joshua's accession, when the Lord had attested his presence with Joshua as with Moses by duplicating the Mosaic signs of victory over the waters and hostile hosts. There Israel was summoned to confirm its consecration to the Lord according to all the words in the Mosaic book of the law and hence to confirm its recognition of Joshua as representative of God's appointment in succession to Moses.

Far from being appendant fragments worked in by an editorial eclectic, the dynastic succession material in Deuteronomy 31-34 treats of that which was the very occasion for the covenant renewal and thus for the whole Book of Deuteronomy. Joshua's succession was the most prominent symbol of Yahweh's continuing theocratic lordship and therefore it was of fundamental and supreme significance in the covenant ceremony and document.[33] By the same token, the Shechem ceremony, as the cultic confirmation of Joshua's succession, emerges as the climactic act in the process of covenant renewal. This explains the appearance of the directions for this final ratification (Deut. 27) at the structural climax of the book, following the stipulations and at the beginning of the section on curses and blessings or covenant ratification. We have placed Deuteronomy 27 in the latter division but it is to be observed that the form is that of commandment and it might well be included with the stipulations. In either case the directions for the covenant ritual on Ebal and Gerizim constitute the central demand and goal of the Deuteronomic treaty. This is the heart of the whole matter and that is why it appears at the heart of the book.[34]

---

33. Noteworthy is Moses' preoccupation with this theme which is manifested in its recurrence at pivotal points in even the earlier chapters: 3:21ff.; 11:29-32; cf. 1:38.

34. It is always easier to criticize ancient texts than to understand them and here again a facile higher criticism has followed the path of least resistance by condemning Deuteronomy 27 as structurally disruptive, a break in the connection between chapters 26 and 28 and certainly "not originally intended for this place" (cf. Wright, op. cit., p. 488). Critics of the prevalent theory that Deuteronomy was designed to promote the centralization of the cultus in Jerusalem have pointed to the awkwardness

It may be observed in passing that Deuteronomy's interest in the perpetuity of Yahweh's rule and specifically its concern with the security of the dynastic succession of Yahweh's vicegerents in Israel is a mark of the profound unity between the Deuteronomic and Davidic covenants. Mendenhall believes there is a fundamental tension between these covenants, the same tension which, as was noted earlier, he finds between the Mosaic and the Abrahamic covenants.[35] Commenting on the discovery of Deuteronomy in Josiah's day, Mendenhall says that "what was rediscovered was not old legislation, but the basic nature of the old amphictyonic covenant. It brought home to Josiah and the religious leadership that they had been living in a fool's paradise in their assumption that Yahweh had irrevocably committed Himself to preserve the nation in the Davidic-Abrahamic covenant. Moses was rediscovered."[36] The resolution of this alleged tension was eventually provided, Mendenhall suggests, in the New Covenant concept by its emphasis on divine forgiveness.

It would seem that a want of theological perspicacity is to blame, at least in part, for Mendenhall's mistranslation of the biblical history into this quite fictional version. For what he interprets as a conflict between covenants is in the last analysis simply the fundamental theological paradox of divine sovereignty and human responsibility which confronts us in all divine-human relationships. Mendenhall has divided between the two aspects of this paradox, both of which are inevitably present in every administration of God's covenants with man, arbitrarily assigning one side of the paradox to the Mosaic covenant and the other side to the Abrahamic-Davidic covenants.

of Deuteronomy's references to Shechem as a cultic site. In order to maintain even a modified version of that theory in the face of such criticism, H. H. Rowley has been obliged to attribute to the supposed late compilers a remarkable degree of political vision and of immunity to religious provincialism and prejudice. (See his "The Prophet Jeremiah and the Book of Deuteronomy" in *Studies in Old Testament Prophecy*, edited by H. H. Rowley, New York, 1950, esp. pp. 165-167.) The untenability of his defense must become the more evident should he attempt to account not merely for the presence but the climactic import of Joshua's Shechemite ceremony within the Deuteronomic treaty.

35. See above, p. 22 J. Bright in his *A History of Israel* (Philadelphia, 1959, esp. pp. 203ff., 300) follows Mendenhall in this misconception, working it out in so thoroughgoing fashion in his reconstruction of the monarchy that it assumes the proportions of a major flaw in his work.

36. *The Biblical Archaeologist*, XVII (1954) 3, p. 73.

Now in the redemptive covenants which are under discussion the divine sovereignty comes to sharpest focus in the promises of blessing to which absolute guarantees are attached, while human responsibility is presupposed in the covenant stipulations, pointedly so in the accompanying threats of curse. Both these elements are present in the Davidic Covenant. For along with its dynastic guarantee, responsibility and judgment are announced (II Sam. 7:14). Nor, on the other hand, is the aspect of guaranteed blessing absent from the Deuteronomic Covenant. In fact, it too contains a divine oath sealing God's promise of redemptive judgment (32:40). And elsewhere in this treaty Moses proclaims the certainty of the covenant renewing grace of God by which his oath-sealed promise to the fathers would be fulfilled to the elect in spite of Israel's covenant-breaking and the visitation of the full vengeance of the covenant upon the guilty (Deut. 4:29-31; 30:1-10; cf. Lev. 26:40-45). Not for the first time at some later stage in Old Testament revelation but here in the Mosaic foundation of the Old Testament canon the prospect of the New Covenant emerges. Moreover, in the divine-human Mediator of this New Covenant there is a manifestation of the unity of the Deuteronomic and Davidic covenants, for it is in him that the promise inherent in the royal commission given the Moses-Joshua dynasty to lead the people of God into their rest is truly fulfilled, just as it is in him and his royal session at the right hand of the Majesty on high that the Davidic dynasty has, according to the divine promise, been established forever.

We are also in a position now to appreciate the fact that the record of Moses' death and of his testamentary blessings on the tribes (Deut. 33, 34) belongs to the original Deuteronomic document. To refer again to Esarhaddon's Nimrud treaty, the essence of it is expressed in the following statement: "*When Esarhaddon, king of Assyria, dies,* you will seat Ashurbanipal, the crown prince, upon the royal throne, he will exercise the kingship (and) lordship of Assyria over you."[37] The dynastic succession stipulation — in effect, the whole covenant since it was concerned solely with dynastic succession — became of force at the death of Esarhaddon. It was the death of the covenant author that caused the covenant stipulations and

37. Translation of Wiseman, *op. cit.,* lines 46-49 (italics ours) ; *cf.* lines 188-191.

sanctions to become operative. That, we would suggest, is the legal key to the understanding of the structural integrity of Deuteronomy 33 and 34 within the context of the whole document. When Moses, Yahweh's mediator-king of Israel, died, an official affixed to the Deuteronomic treaty the notice of that death,[38] so notarizing the covenant in so far as it was (and it was pre-eminently) a covenant designed to enforce Yahweh's royal succession, thereby continuing the lordship of heaven over Israel.

The inclusion in the covenant document of Moses' final blessings upon the tribes (Deut. 33) underscores an important legal datum, namely, the coalescence of the covenantal and testamentary forms. From the viewpoint of the subject people a treaty guaranteeing the suzerain's dynastic succession is an expression of their covenantal relation to their over-lord; but from the viewpoint of the loyal son(s) of the suzerain the arrangement is testamentary. Testament and suzerainty covenant are not simple equivalents but to the extent that the latter is concerned with dynastic succession it is informed by the primary administrative principle of the testament — it is not in force while the testator lives.

From Joshua's point of view as heir appointive over Israel the Book of Deuteronomy as a whole was a Mosaic testament. But Deuteronomy 33 is a testament to which all Israel was beneficiary. This compels us to reckon with another facet in the multiform religious relationship of Israel with Yahweh. Israel's divine election was unto adoption as well as unto the giving of the law (Rom. 9:4). The Israelites were, therefore, sons as well as servants (cf. Ex. 4:22; Deut. 14:1) and Moses as God's representative was unto them as father as well as king. Moreover, as sons of the heavenly King, they were all heirs to a royal reign. Indeed, the establishment of Israel as a royal priesthood over Canaan was in a figure a reinstatement of man as vicegerent of God over Paradise. At the same time, though the concept of all God's people participating in Moses' gifts and functions comes to expression even in the Pentateuch (Num. 11:16ff., esp. v. 29; cf. Deut. 34:9), Israel the heir was under

---

38. This official could also well have been responsible for certain brief paragraphs which were not parts of the covenant ceremony conducted by Moses but purely documentary formulations added to round out the treaty pattern; e.g., the preamble (1:1-5) or a passage like 4:44-49, which labels a treaty section. Cf. G. T. Manley, *The Book of the Law*, London, 1957, pp. 150-162.

governors until the time appointed of the Father (Gal. 4:1, 2). The emphasis remained on servanthood rather than sonship until New Covenant times (*cf*. Gal. 4:7; Rom. 8:17).

Several New Testament passages which deal expressly with covenant administration might be profitably re-examined in the light of the new evidence, particularly, Hebrews 9:16, 17. The problem in that passage has been that it appeared illogical to establish principles of covenantal administration by appeal to procedures governing testamentary dispositions since the two seemed to be totally distinct legal forms. If, however, one might assume that the author's parenthetical allusion in these verses is to the dynastic-testamentary aspect of ancient suzerainty covenants and especially of the Old Covenant as exemplified by Deuteronomy, the way would be open to a satisfactory solution. Hebrews is, of course, pervasively occupied with a comparison of the covenants mediated by Jesus and Moses but it is also significant that one of its recurrent themes is dynastic appointment and perpetuity (*cf*. 1:2ff., 8; 5:6ff.; 6:20ff.), the precise area of covenantal administration for which the merging of the covenantal and the testamentary is attested. If that is indeed the area of reference in Hebrews 9:16, 17, the picture suggested would be that of Christ's children (*cf*. 2:13) inheriting his universal dominion as their eternal portion (note 9:15b; *cf*. also, 1:14; 2:5ff.; 6:17; 11:7ff.). And such is the wonder of the messianic Mediator-Testator that the royal inheritance of his sons, which becomes of force only through his death, is nevertheless one of co-regency with the living Testator! For (to follow the typological direction provided by Heb. 9:16, 17 according to the present interpretation) Jesus is both dying Moses and succeeding Joshua. Not merely after a figure but in truth a royal Mediator *redivivus*, he secures the divine dynasty by succeeding himself in resurrection power and ascension glory.

In the light of the evidence now surveyed, it would seem indisputable that the Book of Deuteronomy, not in the form of some imaginary original core but precisely in the integrity of its present form, the only one for which there is any objective evidence, exhibits the structure of the ancient suzerainty treaties in the unity and completeness of their classic pattern. That there should be a measure of oratorical and literary enrichment of the traditional legal form is natural, considering the caliber of the author and the grandeur of the occasion. And, of course, there is the conceptual adaptation inevitable in the adoption of common formal media for the expression of the unique revelation of God in the Scriptures. What is remarkable is the detailed extent to which God has utilized this legal instrument of human kingdoms for the definition and administration of his own redemptive reign over his people.

The implication of the new evidence for the questions of the antiquity and authenticity of Deuteronomy must not be suppressed. The kind of document with which Deuteronomy has been identified did not originate in some recurring ritual situation. These treaties were of course prepared for particular historical occasions. It is necessary, therefore, to seek for an appropriate historical episode in the national life of Israel in order to account satisfactorily for the origin of the Deuteronomic treaty. Without now rehearsing all the data that make it perfectly apparent that the addressees were the recently founded theocratic nation, we would press only one question: Where, either in monarchic or pre-monarchic times, except in the very occasion to which Deuteronomy traces itself can an historical situation be found in which the twelve tribes would have been summoned to a covenantal engagement whose peculiar purpose was, as the purpose of the Deuteronomic treaty demonstrably was, to guarantee the continuance of a (non-Davidic) dynasty over Israel?

Another index of the time of Deuteronomy's composition is provided by the evolution of the documentary form of suzerainty treaties. Admittedly the available evidence is still quite limited and the differences among the extant treaties are not to be exaggerated. It is indeed one species that we meet throughout Old Testament times. Nevertheless, there is a discernible evolution.[39] For example, where the beginning is preserved in the first millennium B.C. treaties of Sefireh and Nimrud, it is not the opening *umma* of the second millennium B.C. Hittite treaties, or its equivalent. Also, in the Sefireh treaties only a trace remains of the blessing sanctions which are prominent in the earlier treaties, and the sanctions in Esarhaddon's treaties consist exclusively of curses. The most remarkable

39. W. F. Albright (*From the Stone Age to Christianity* (Second Edition), New York, 1957, p. 16) asserts that the structure of the later treaties "is quite different" than the Syro-Anatolian treaties of the fourteenth-thirteenth centuries B.C. For a cautious statement of the case see J. L'Hour, "L'Alliance de Sichem," *Revue Biblique*, LXIX (Jan. 1962) 1, p. 15.

difference is that the historical prologue, the distinctive second section of the second millennium treaties, is no longer found in the later texts.

Accordingly, while it is necessary to recognize a substantial continuity in pattern between the earlier and later treaties, it is proper to distinguish the Hittite treaties of the second millennium B.C. as the "classic" form. And without any doubt the Book of Deuteronomy belongs to the classic stage in this documentary evolution. Here then is significant confirmation of the prima facie case for the Mosaic origin of the Deuteronomic treaty of the great King.

The literary genre of Deuteronomy also has important implications for the way in which, having once been produced, this document would have been transmitted to subsequent generations. By their very nature treaties like Deuteronomy were inviolable. They were sealed legal contracts. Indeed, as has already been observed, it was standard practice to deposit such treaties in sanctuaries under the eye of the oath deities.

There are, moreover, interesting examples in some of the extant texts of specific curses pronounced against anyone who would in any way violate the treaty inscriptions. Referring to the treaty-tablet, which bore the seal of Ashur, Esarhaddon declared: "(You swear that) you will not alter (it), you will not consign (it) to the fire nor throw (it) into the water, nor [bury (it)] in the earth nor destroy it by any cunning device, nor make [(it) disappear], nor sweep (it) away. (If you do,) [may Ashur, king of the] gods who decrees the fates, [decree for you] evil and not good."[40]

Similarly a special curse is included in the Sefireh I and II treaties against anyone responsible for effacing the inscriptions from their steles.[41] The sacredness of the treaty steles is en-

---

40. Lines 410-415a; the translation is that of D. J. Wiseman, *The Vassal-Treaties of Esarhaddon*, p. 60. *Cf.* lines 397ff. The description of the series of actions by which the tablet might be destroyed corresponds remarkably to the description of Moses' treatment of the stone tables of the covenant and the golden calf in Ex. 32:19b, 20. It would seem clear that these actions were not merely the impulsive expression of Moses' wrath but rather constituted a standard symbolic procedure for declaring a covenant broken. The enforced drinking of the powder-strewn water represented the exposure of the guilty to the threatened curses of the covenant. Compare the jealousy ordeal of Num. 5:23, 24 in which it is again a matter of a broken vow.

41. See Sefireh I, Face C, 17ff. and Sefireh II, Face C, 1ff.

hanced in the curse of Sefireh II by designating them "the houses of the gods" (*bty 'lhy'*) or "bethels."[42]

Corresponding to these special stele curses is the injunction of Deuteronomy 4:2a, set in a context of covenant sanctions: "Ye shall not add unto the word which I command you, neither shall ye diminish *ought* from it."[43]

These facts stand in diametrical opposition to the whole modern approach to the Book of Deuteronomy. According to the current speculations Deuteronomy was produced by an extended process of modification and enlargement of a pliable tradition. The most relevant evidence, however, indicates that once they had been prepared for a particular historical occasion, documents like Deuteronomy would not be susceptible to ready modification. They were in fact protected from all alteration, erasure, and expansion by the most specific, solemn, and severe sanctions. And the force of these facts is intensified in the case of the Deuteronomic treaty by the reverence which the Israelites will have had for it not simply as a sealed and sanctioned covenant but as in truth the very word of God revealed to them from heaven.

Now that the form critical data compel the recognition of the antiquity not merely of this or that element within Deuteronomy but of the Deuteronomic treaty in its integrity, any persistent insistence on a final edition of the book around the seventh century B.C. can be nothing more than a vestigial hypothesis, no longer performing a significant function in Old Testament criticism. Is it too much to hope that modern higher criticism's notorious traditionalism will no longer prove inertial enough to prevent the Deuteronomic bark from setting sail once more for its native port?

---

42. A comparison has naturally been made with the pillar associated with Jacob's covenantal vow, which he said should be "God's house," Gen. 28:18-22; cf. J. A. Fitzmyer, "The Aramaic Inscriptions of Sefire I and II," *Journal of the American Oriental Society* 81 (August-September, 1961) 3, p. 214. This covenant-bethel phenomenon also invites attention to the fundamental character of the altar in Israel as the dwelling place of Yahweh where he recorded his covenant name, and beyond the Old Testament altar to the Christ, who in his incarnation was given for a covenant of the people (Isa. 42:6; 49:8) and was at once the temple and the Word of God. Cf., too, Ex. 24:4ff; Deut. 27:4-8; Josh. 8:30ff.; 24:25-27.

43. Cf. Deut. 12:32; Rev. 22:18, 19; and the familiar boast of Josephus in *Contra Apionem* 1:8.

PART II

A COMMENTARY ON
THE DEUTERONOMIC TREATY

1. Introduction and Outline

INTRODUCTION

The English title of the Book of Deuteronomy is apparently based on the LXX's mistranslation of the phrase, "a copy of this law" (17:18), as *to deuteronomion touto*, "this second law." The Jewish title, *devārîm*, "words," arises from the custom of using the opening word(s) of a book as its name; the opening statement in Deuteronomy is: "These are the words which Moses spake" (1:1a, ASV). Since ancient suzerainty treaties began similarly, the Jewish title draws attention to one of the clues which identify the literary character of this book.

The origin of Deuteronomy is of crucial significance in modern higher critical study of the Pentateuch and indeed in studies of Old Testament literature and theology in general. According to the older Developmental Hypothesis, Deuteronomy originated in the seventh century B.C. and was the basis for Josiah's reform (*cf.* II Kgs. 22:3-23:25), allegedly in the interests of a centralized cultus (*cf.* commentary on 12:4-14). That view in modified forms continues among negative critics, but some would suggest a post-exilic date and others trace the Deuteronomic legislation to the early monarchic and even pre-monarchic period. Significant for the dating of the several alleged documents of the Pentateuch is the tendency to explain the supposed conflict of their codes not by resort to a long chronological evolution but by positing a different geographic-cultic provenance for each of them. Deuteronomy in particular is then traced to a Shechemite sanctuary. Instead of associating Deuteronomy with the first four books of the Pentateuch, one modern approach thinks in terms of a Tetrateuch and of a Deuteronomic literary-historical tradition comprising Deuteronomy through II Kings.

Current orthodox Christian scholarship joins older Christian and Jewish tradition in accepting the plain claims of Deuteronomy itself to be the farewell, ceremonial addresses of Moses to the Israelite assembly in the plains of Moab. Deuteronomy 31:9 and 24 state that Moses wrote as well as spoke "the words of this law." A theocratic officer completed the document by recording Moses' death (chap. 34) and probably Moses' Wit-

47

ness Song (chap. 32) and testament (chap. 33). Possibly he also added certain other brief skeletal elements to this legal document.

The unity and authenticity of Deuteronomy as a Mosaic product are confirmed by the remarkable conformity of its structure to that of the suzerainty type of covenant or treaty in its classic, mid-second millennium B.C. form. (See above, Part I, Chapter 2, and consult the following commentary for details.)

It is only within the framework of the administration of God's redemptive covenant that Deuteronomy can be adequately interpreted. The covenant promises given to the patriarchs and finally and truly fulfilled in Christ had a provisional and typical fulfillment in the covenants mediated to Israel through Moses. In the Sinaitic Covenant the theocracy was established, with Moses as earthly representative of Yahweh's kingship over Israel. Then, when the rebellious exodus generation had perished in the wilderness and Moses' own death was imminent, it was necessary to renew the covenant to the second generation. The central, decisive act of the ceremony was the consecration of the servant people by an oath to their divine Lord. In particular, God's reign as symbolically represented in the earthly, mediatorial dynasty must be confirmed by securing from Israel a commitment to obey Joshua as the successor to Moses in that dynasty.

Part of the standard procedure followed in the ancient Near East when "the great king" gave his covenant to a vassal people was the preparation of a text of the ceremony as the treaty document and witness. The Book of Deuteronomy is the document prepared by Moses as a witness to the dynastic covenant which the Lord gave to Israel in the plains of Moab (*cf.* 31:26).

OUTLINE OF DEUTERONOMY

I. Preamble: Covenant Mediator, 1:1-5

II. Historical Prologue: Covenant History, 1:6-4:49
    A. From Horeb to Hormah, 1:6-2:1
    B. Advance to the Arnon, 2:2-23
    C. Conquest of Transjordania, 2:24-3:29
    D. Summary of the Covenant, 4:1-49

III. Stipulations: Covenant Life, 5:1-26:19
    A. The Great Commandment, 5:1-11:32
      1. God's Covenant Lordship, 5:1-33

2. Commentary

I. Preamble: Covenant Mediator, 1:1-5

Ancient suzerainty treaties began with a preamble in which the speaker, the one who was declaring his lordship and demanding the vassal's allegiance, identified himself. The Deuteronomic preamble identifies the speaker as Moses (v. 1a), but Moses as the earthly, mediatorial representative of Yahweh (v. 3b), the heavenly Suzerain and ultimate Lord of this covenant.

1:1-5. *These are the words* (v. 1a). It was with such an introductory formula that the extra-biblical treaties began. The site of the covenant renewal ceremony of which Deuteronomy is the documentary witness was the Jordan area in the land of Moab (vv. 1a, 5a; *cf.* 4:44-46). The time was the last month of the fortieth year after the exodus (v. 3a) when the men of war of that generation had all perished (*cf.* 2:16), the conquest of Transjordania was accomplished (v. 4; *cf.* 2:24ff.), and the time of Moses' death was at hand. It was especially this last circumstance that occasioned the renewal of the covenant. The Lord secured continuity of the mediatorial dynasty by requiring of Israel a pledge of obedience to his new appointee, Joshua (*cf.* 31:3; 34:9), and a new vow of consecration to himself. The ceremony is described as a declaration or exposition of *this law* (v. 5) since the stipulations occupied so central and extensive a place in suzerainty covenants.

The location of this assembly is apparently further described in verse 2b. Although the mention of otherwise unknown localities makes interpretation uncertain, the purpose of the notation in verses 1b, 2 seems to be to orient the Moab assembly historically as much as geographically by indicating that it lay at the end of the journey from Horeb via the Arabah wilderness. For Israel the journey to Canaan by this route proved to be of forty years duration (v. 3), although the original route they followed to Paran was normally only an eleven-day trek (v. 2). At Paran on the southern border of Canaan, however, Israel had rebelled, refusing to enter the land (*cf.* Num. 12:16ff.), and so that generation had been sentenced to die in the wilderness. Now their children had arrived via the Arabah route from "Suph" (presumably the Gulf of Aqabah) for an eastern approach to Canaan through the land of Moab. Both the direction of approach to Canaan and the length of the wanderings spoke of a history of covenant breaking and of postponed inheritance. There is thus an interesting contrast between the preamble's look south from Moab into the past of failure and curse and Moses' closing look north from Moab into Israel's future of fulfillment and blessing (*cf.* 34:1-4).

II. Historical Prologue: Covenant History, 1:6-4:49

Following the preamble in the international suzerainty treaties there was an historical section, written in an I-thou style, which surveyed the previous relationships of lord and vassal. Its purpose was to establish the historical justification for the lord's continuing reign. Benefits allegedly conferred by the lord upon the vassal were cited with a view to grounding the vassal's allegiance in a sense of gratitude complementary to the sense of fear which the preamble's grandiose identification of the suzerain had been calculated to inspire. When treaties were renewed, the historical prologue was brought up to date. All these formal features characterize Deuteronomy 1:6-4:49.

The historical prologue of the Sinaitic Covenant had referred to the deliverance from Egypt (Ex. 20:2b). Deuteronomy begins at the scene of the Sinaitic Covenant and continues the history up to the covenant renewal assembly in Moab, emphasizing the recent Transjordanian victories. When, still later, Joshua again renewed the covenant to Israel, he continued the narrative in his historical prologue through the events of his own leadership of Israel, the conquest and the settlement in Canaan (*cf.* Josh. 24:2-13)

A. From Horeb to Hormah, 1:6-2:1.

1:6-8. By the end of a year's encampment in the Sinai area, where the covenant was ratified and the tabernacle established as God's dwelling in Israel, the time had come for the next decisive step in the fulfillment of the promises made to the fathers (vv. 6, 8b). *Turn you . . . go in and possess the land* (vv. 7, 8). The initiative in the advance against the land of promised possession was provided by the Lord's command (*cf.* Num. 10:11-13). On verse 7b, *cf.* Genesis 15:18ff.

1:9-18. With the hour of his death at hand, Moses was concerned to confirm the authority of those who must bear the burden of rule after him. Of primary importance was the succession of Joshua, to which he would presently refer (*cf.* 1:38; 3:21, 28); but here Moses reminds Israel of the authorization of other judicial officers. For the original account, see Exodus 18:13ff. The very circumstance that gave rise to the need for these judicial assistants to Moses, namely, the multiplication of Abraham's seed as the stars of heaven (v. 10), was itself evidence of the Lord's faithfulness in fulfilling his covenantal promises (*cf.* Gen. 12:2; 15:5; *etc.*) and thus afforded encouragement to Israel to advance in faith to take possession of Canaan (*cf.* 1:7, 8). God's faithful mediator, reflecting the goodness of his Lord, prays for the full realization of all the promises of the Abrahamic Covenant (v. 11). *For the judgment is God's* (v. 17). This reason for righteous administration of justice is at the same time a reminder of the theocratic nature of the Israelite kingdom, a reminder that God was the lord who was making covenant anew with them this day.

1:19-40. Over against the covenant faithfulness of the Lord (*cf.* 1:6-18) there had been the infidelity and disobedience of Israel. The fact that the Lord was renewing his covenant against this background of the vassal's past rebellions further magnified his grace and goodness (*cf.* the introductory comments on II. Historical Prologue).

The particular sin of the people of Israel recalled on the eve of their conquest of Canaan was their refusal to advance into Canaan on the first occasion when they were commanded to do so some thirty-eight years earlier. For the original account, see Numbers 13 and 14. At that time Israel's approach to Canaan had been from the south (v. 19). Moses clearly advised them that Canaan was theirs for the taking (vv. 20, 21; *cf.* 1:7, 8; Gen. 15:16); yet when so ordered by the Lord (*cf.* Num. 13:1ff.), he consented to Israel's strategy of reconnaissance before attack (vv. 22-25). *Ye rebelled against the commandment of the Lord* (v. 26). Israel's response to the report of the spies was one of faithless fear and refusal to advance (vv. 26-28). Their perversity went to the extreme of interpreting their election as an expression of God's hatred of them; he had delivered them from the Egyptians only that the Canaanites might kill them (v. 27)! *Ye did not believe the Lord* (v. 32). They could not be dissuaded from their open revolt against the Lord's covenant program by all Moses' pleas, even though he assured them that God would vouchsafe to them fatherly and supernatural help like that which they had experienced both in Egypt and in the wilderness (vv. 29-33). *The Lord heard . . . and was wroth* (v. 34). Their unbelief provoked the divine verdict, sealed by an oath, sentencing them to exile from the homeland which they had refused to enter, exile unto death in the wilderness (vv. 34-40). In this announcement of judgment there was a manifestation of God's covenant mercy, for not only the godly spies Caleb and Joshua were to be spared to enter Canaan at a later day, but the whole second generation of Israel as well (v. 39). Therein lay the promise of a gracious new beginning — now being fulfilled in the Deuteronomic covenant renewal.

The Lord was angry with me for your sakes (v. 37). Israel's rebelliousness eventually became the occasion for a failure on Moses' part to fulfill properly his high mediatorial calling as a type of the messianic Mediator who is always perfectly submissive to the Father's will (*cf.* 3:26; 4:21; 32:50ff.). This event took place at the return to Kadesh after thirty-eight years wandering (*cf.* Num. 20:1ff.). It is mentioned here in connection with the beginning of the wanderings because its consequence was that Moses had to share with the older generation in their exclusion from Canaan (*cf.* v. 35). *Joshua the son of Nun, which standeth before thee, he shall go in thither* (v. 38). The disqualification of Moses necessitated the appointment of Joshua as heir to the mediatorial dynasty to lead the spared *little ones* into Canaan (v. 39).

1:41-2:1. After Israel had capped their revolt against the Lord's will with a presumptuous and disastrous assault on Canaan in the vain hope of escaping God's verdict against them (1:41-44; *cf.* Num. 14:40ff.), they remained a while in Kadesh (1:46). Then, as God had commanded (1:40; *cf.* Num. 14:25), they wandered unto their wilderness graves (2:1a). So the time was spent in the area to the southwest of the Edomites until the fortieth year (2:1b; *cf.* 2:14-16).

B. ADVANCE TO THE ARNON, 2:2-23

2:2-8. *Cf.* Numbers 20:14-21. *Turn you northward* (v. 3b). The divine mandate to advance on Canaan given a generation earlier (*cf.* 2:14-16) was once again sounded. On the route, apparently around the north of Edom and across the way of the Arabah which leads from the Gulf of Aqabah to the Dead Sea, see Numbers 20:21ff.; 21:1-12; 33:36-44. Uncertainty as to the route arises from our inability to identify many of the sites, but it is not probable that Deuteronomy 2:8 or Numbers 21:4 suggests a southern detour as far as the Gulf of Aqabah as part of a circuit of Mount Seir. *Ye are to pass through the border of your brethren the children of Esau* (v. 4, ASV). Jacob and

Esau confront each other again. The struggle for the birthright, however, was long since settled; Canaan was Jacob's. Nevertheless, Esau had his possession, too, in Mount Seir (*cf.* Gen. 36) and Israel was forbidden to contend for it (v. 5). (See 23:7, 8 for the relatively privileged position of the Edomites in Israel's assembly.) When the policy dictated by the Lord was followed, the Edomites refused passage through their land, thus compelling a circuit about their borders (v. 8; *cf.* Num. 20:14ff.). Esau's fear of Israel (v. 4; contrast Gen. 32:3ff.) was displayed by his blocking entry into Seir (Num. 20:20). The Numbers passage does not say that the Edomites refused to sell provisions to the Israelites once it was clear that Israel was content to go around Edom. Moreover, Deuteronomy 2:6 and 29 do not clearly state that Edom did sell provisions to Israel. For even 2:29a possibly refers only to the last clause in verse 28 (compare 2:29b with 23:3, 4). Hence there is no contradiction between Numbers and Deuteronomy on this matter. *These forty years the Lord thy God hath been with thee* (v. 7) — another reminder of God's past benevolences, bestowed on his underserving vassal even during the execution of his judgment of exile (*cf. e.g.,* 32:1).

2:9-23. Israel came into contact next with the descendants of Abraham's nephew Lot, the Moabites and Ammonites (*cf.* Gen. 19:37, 38). *Do not harass Moab or contend with them in battle* (v. 9, RSV). Though these groups did not enjoy the Edomites' privilege of entrance into Israel's assembly (*cf.* 23:3ff.), they, too, had possessions for which Israel was not to contend (*cf.* vv. 5, 19). Each nation had dispossessed a tall Anakim-like people usually known as Rephaim but called Emim by the Moabites (vv. 10, 11) and Zamzummim by the Ammonites (vv. 20, 21. *Cf.* Gen. 14:5). The tribe of Anak is mentioned in Egyptian execration texts and the Rephaim in Ugaritic administrative texts. *The Horites also dwelt in Seir aforetime* (v. 12, ASV). In connection with the territorial acquisitions of each nation it is noted that similarly the Lord had dispossessed the earlier Horite, *i.e.,* Hurrian, population of Seir in favor of the Edomites (vv. 12a, 22; *cf.* v. 5b). Added to that notice in each case is one further historical illustration: the Lord's bestowal of an inheritance on Israel (v. 12b), and, in the second case, the dispossession of the Avvim by the Caphtorim (v. 23). If the comparison with Israel's conquest of their land (v. 12b) was not appended by someone like the official who evidently completed the Deuteronomic document after Moses' death, the reference would be to the conquest of Transjordania.

By all these historical notices the covenant servant Israel was advised that Yahweh, their great King, had an hegemony over the territory about their promised land. In his all-controlling providence he had repeatedly dispossessed great nations — even the Anakim, whose presence in Canaan had frightened Israel into rebellion against him a generation before (*cf.* 1:28; 2:14, 15). And he had done so in behalf of various peoples who enjoyed no such special status of covenant calling as elect Israel had received. With what confidence, therefore, Israel might obey Yahweh's summons to rise up and cross the mountain torrents of Zered (v. 13) and Arnon (v. 24), and soon the Jordan (*cf.* Josh. 1:2). See Amos 9:7 for another lesson drawn from such historical data. The Zered (v. 13) marked the southern boundary of Moab along whose eastern border Israel went, so approaching the frontiers of Ammon, which lay east and north of Moab (vv. 18, 19; *cf.* v. 8b; Num. 21:11ff.).

C. Conquest of Transjordania, 2:24-3:29

2:24-3:11. Across the Arnon (2:24), Moab's northern boundary, Israel would encounter Amorites. Sihon the Amorite ruled from the Arnon to the Jabbok (2:36; *cf.* Num. 21:24) with his capital at Heshbon (2:26), and Og the Amorite (*cf.* 3:8) ruled from the Jabbok over northern Gilead and Bashan to Mount Hermon (3:4, 8-10; *cf.* 3:13; Josh. 12:5). The Amorites were protected by no such inviolability as the Edomites, Moabites, and Ammonites. The fact that an offer of peace was made to Sihon (2:26) indicates that his land in Transjordania (which had earlier belonged to the Moabites and Ammonites, *cf.* Josh. 13:25; 21:26; Jud. 11:13) was not a part of Israel's promised land proper (*cf.* Deut. 20:10). But his people, as a people of Canaan, fell under the *ḥērem* principle (see comments on 7:1-5 and *cf.* 2:33-35; 3:6; 7:2, 16; 20:14-17). It was indeed the time when the Amorites should have ripened for judgment which had been set as the hour for Israel's conquest of Canaan (*cf.* Gen. 15:16). With the spread of these Amorites across the Jordan there was a corresponding extension of the territory that would fall into Israel's possession by conquest.

Therefore, a new divine order met Israel at the Arnon: *Begin to take possession and contend* (v. 24, RSV). And a new divine promise: *This day will I begin to put the dread of thee . . .*

upon the nations (v. 25). The process of Sihon's fall was much the same as that of Amenophis II, the pharaoh of the exodus. Each was approached with a request to favor the Israelites (2:26-29), which he refused because the Lord hardened his heart (2:30). Each made a hostile advance against Israel (2:32) and suffered defeat as the Lord fought for his people (2:31, 33ff.). On 2:29, *cf.* comments on 2:2-8. The upper course of the Jabbok to the east ran north and south separating Sihon's kingdom from the Ammonites (2:37). *The Lord our God delivered him before us* (2:33). In this victory, the beginning of the dispossession of the Amorites, there were demonstrated the irresistible power (v. 36) and absolute authority (v. 37) of Yahweh's covenant lordship exercised over and in behalf of Israel. For the original account of the conquest of Sihon, see Numbers 21:21ff.

Fear him not: for I will deliver him . . . into thy hand (3:2). The advance against Og was also at God's command, accompanied by his promise of success (*cf.* 2:24, 25), and victory was again the gift of Yahweh (3:3). Neither the height of the enemy's fortifications (v. 5) nor the height of their king (v. 11; *cf.* 2:11, 20) was to arouse fear in the armies of the Lord. On the conquest of Og, see also Numbers 21:33ff. 3:8-11 summarizes the fruits of Israel's victories at Jahaz (2:32) and Edrei (3:1).

3:12-20. It was given to Moses to witness the beginning of both the conquest and the distribution of the tribal allotments. For the latter event, see Numbers 32. The initiative in requesting the newly conquered land was taken by the tribes of Reuben and Gad. But when Moses granted the request, he took account of particular triumphs gained in the north by the Manassite families of Machir, Jair, and Nobah (v. 14; *cf.* Num. 32:39-42). To this half tribe of Manasseh was given the territory of Og, *i.e.*, Gilead north from the Jabbok and Bashan (vv. 13, 15; *cf.* Josh. 13:29-31). To Reuben and Gad was given Sihon's land from the Jabbok in Gilead south to the Arnon, the tribe of Gad being located north of Reuben, with their boundary just above the Dead Sea. Gad also received the Jordan valley as far as the Sea of Chinnereth (vv. 12, 16, 17; *cf.* Josh. 13:15-28). *Ye shall pass over armed before your brethren* (v. 18). The strict condition of the two and a half tribes inheriting land outside of Canaan was that they first fulfill their responsible share in the conquest of Canaan (*cf.* Num. 32:6-32). Moses' intense concern for this matter emerges again here in the Deuteronomic treaty (vv. 18-20).

3:21-29. Except for the covenant renewal ceremony itself, the conquest and distribution of the land beyond Jordan eastward brought Moses' work there to an end. *O Lord God, thou hast begun to show thy servant thy greatness* (v. 24). In these achievements the servant of God had witnessed the earnest of Israel's entrance upon its inheritance. Much, however, as he longed to see the fulfillment of God's promises in the goodly land of Canaan itself (v. 25), he was not permitted to pass across but only to look across the Jordan (v. 27; cf. Num. 27: 12ff.; Deut. 34:1ff.). On verse 26, cf. 1:37; 4:21f. *But charge Joshua . . . for he shall go over before this people* (v. 28). Moses' final duty was to charge the people to conquer in the name of the Lord (v. 22) and to commission Joshua to lead them in that conquest, strong in the confidence that the Lord who had begun a good work for them would also perfect it (vv. 21, 28; cf. Num. 27:18-23; Deut. 1:38; 31:7, 8, 14, 23). The reference to Beth-peor in the identification of the site of these final acts of Moses (v. 29; cf. 4:46) recalls other events that transpired during Israel's encampment there (cf. Num. 22-25).

D. SUMMARY OF THE COVENANT, 4:1-49

The historical prologue closes with exhortation. This is transitional to the following section on the obligations of the covenant relationship. The summons to obedience sounded here is briefly echoed in paragraphs that introduce significant divisions within the stipulations (see 5:1; 6:1; 12:1). Deuteronomy 4 is remarkable in that it embodies to some extent all the features which constitute the documentary pattern of suzerainty treaties. Within it are the identification of the Author of the covenant as speaker (vv. 1, 2, 5, 10), references to past historical relations, the presentation of the central demand for pure devotion to the Suzerain, appeal to the sanctions of blessing and curse, invocation of witnesses (v. 26), the requirement to transmit the knowledge of the covenant to subsequent generations (vv. 9, 10), and allusion to the dynastic issue (vv. 21, 22). This mingling of the several leading aspects of covenant institution found here and elsewhere throughout the book is explained by the origin of the material in the free oratory of Moses' farewell. Deuteronomy is not a document prepared in the state office with dispassionate adherence to legal form.

4:1-8. A Call to Wisdom. The statutes that Moses taught Israel were a revelation of the will of God (v. 5). They must not, therefore, suffer amendment or abridgement through human legislation: *Ye shall not add unto the word which I command you, neither shall ye diminish ought from it* (v. 2; cf. 12:32; Rev. 22:18ff.). Similarly, some of the secular treaties prohibit, under threat of curse, any tampering with the treaty inscription (see above, p. 43). Man's whole obligation is to heed, and to the obedient Israelite was given the promise of life and rich inheritance (v. 1). The fact that ultimately piety and prosperity will be united was foreshadowed in the history of the Israelite theocracy, for it symbolized the consummate kingdom of God. Illustrative of this principle was the divine judgment on Israel's involvement in the idolatry of the Baal of Peor (v. 3; Num. 25:1-9), in that those who proved faithful in that temptation were spared the plague of death (v. 4). Understandably then, obedience to God's law is identified as true wisdom: *this is your wisdom and your understanding in the sight of the nations* (v. 6). Obedience is the way to the enjoyment of the supreme blessings of the covenant — the nearness of God in saving power (v. 7) and knowledge of true righteousness (v. 8). This light revealed in Israel has indeed become the light of the Gentiles (v. 6b). In this exposition of the way of the covenant as the way of wisdom (vv. 6-8), the foundation was laid in the Torah for the Wisdom literature which was afterwards to find its place in the sacred canon.

4:9-31. The Folly of Idolatry. As Moses confronted the new generation with the challenge of reaffirming the allegiance to Yahweh pledged by their fathers at Sinai, he was vividly mindful of the fathers' sin of the golden calf by which they had violated the covenant almost immediately after it had been sealed (cf. 9:7ff.; Ex. 32). He therefore stressed the prohibition contained in the second commandment as he contrasted to the way of wisdom and life (cf. 4:1-8) the way of folly and destruction.

The day that thou stoodest before the Lord thy God in Horeb (v. 10). At Horeb God had revealed to Israel the manner of true worship (vv. 10ff.). That revelation was contained in the covenant which was first orally communicated and then inscribed on the two tables. The preparation of duplicate documents, one for the suzerain and one for the vassal, was the regular procedure in ratifying suzerainty treaties (see above,

Chapter 1). The fact that the contents of the tables are called the "ten commandments" as well as "covenant" points to the nature of the covenant as a declaration of Yahweh's lordship. *The Lord spake unto you out of the midst of the fire: ye heard the voice of the words, but saw no similitude* (v. 12). The manner of true worship was revealed by the very nature of the theophany (vv. 12, 15). For though a voice was heard declaring the words of the covenant, no form of God was seen but only the devouring fire of God's glory. The visible symbols of God's self-revelation thus re-enforced the prohibition of the second commandment.

Israel was to beware of the idolatry of worshiping *a graven image* (v. 16), the work of men's hands (vv. 16-18, 23; *cf.* 5:8), but also the idolatry of worshiping the work of God's hands, *the host of heaven* (v. 19). The worship of the visible and creaturely was characteristic of the nations, whom God had abandoned unto their perverse folly (v. 19b; *cf.* 29:26; Rom. 1:21ff.). *But the Lord hath taken you . . . to be unto him a people of inheritance* (v. 20). For Israel to turn aside into idolatry was to prefer the lot of reprobation to her divine election as God's own redeemed and exclusive possession (*cf.* 7:6; 14:2), an exclusive privilege which required an exclusive service and devotion. *Take heed unto yourselves, lest ye forget the covenant of the Lord your God* (v. 23). Prophetically Moses warned that prolonged enjoyment of the blessings of Canaan, blessings denied even to him (vv. 21, 22a), would produce the forgetfulness of old age (v. 25; *cf.* v. 9). Let Israel, therefore, recall that the God to whom its allegiance was sworn at Sinai appeared there as a consuming fire (v. 24). If provoked to jealousy by idolatry he will visit the covenant curses on such folly — and what greater curse than to abandon the repudiators of divine election to the vanity of the idolatry they preferred and to the community of men of like reprobate mind and destiny (vv. 27, 28; *cf.* 28:64ff.)? Nevertheless, God's covenant with Israel is one of salvation and a realization of its blessings is guaranteed by the oath of God to the patriarchs (v. 31). *If from thence thou shalt seek the Lord thy God, thou shalt find him* (v. 29). After Israel's folly and judgment God will grant repentance so that beyond the curse of exile there may arise in the latter days the blessings of restoration (vv. 29-31; *cf.* 30:1ff.).

4:32-40. Evidences of True Religion. *Unto thee it was showed, that thou mightest know that the Lord he is God; there is none else beside him* (v. 35). The identity of Yahweh as God alone, sovereign Creator of heaven and earth, was evidenced by his wondrous self-revelations in theophany and redemptive miracle (vv. 35, 36; *cf.* Ex. 10:2). His glorious acts at Horeb (v. 33) and in Egypt (v. 34) were signs without parallel; no idol of the nations ever thus identified itself (vv. 32ff.). *Because he loved thy fathers* (v. 37). If the purpose of Israel's calling was to bring them to reverent fear and knowledge of Yahweh as God, the source of that calling was found in God's free grace (*cf.* 9:5). Moses traced the deliverance from Egypt and inheritance of the promised rest (earnest of which was the occupation of Transjordania) to God's sovereign love of the patriarchs, first of all, of Abraham (vv. 37, 38). These miraculous mercies of the past and the hope of the covenant's felicity in the future (v. 40) were urged as reasons for conscientious reckoning with the claims of Yahweh's exclusive deity (vv. 39, 40a).

4:41-43. As part of the historical prologue of the Deuteronomic treaty, the most recent significant event in God's gracious government of Israel was cited. In obedience to God's direction (*cf.* Num. 35:1, 14), Moses appointed three cities of refuge in Israel's Transjordanian inheritance, one each in the southern, central, and northern sectors (*cf.* 19:1-13).

4:44-49. This passage is transitional. As a summary of the Transjordanian conquests (vv. 46b-49; *cf.* 2:32-36; 3:1-17) it serves as a conclusion to the historical prologue. But it is also immediately introductory to the stipulations (vv. 44-46a). The scene of the covenant ceremony and Moses' farewell is precisely set (*cf.* 1:3-5; 3:29). The temporal clause, *When they came forth out of Egypt* (v. 46, ASV), marks the covenantal transaction as belonging to the Mosaic era of prolonged journeying from Egypt to the Jordan. The ratifying of this covenant was to be finally concluded in the new era when Israel entered into Canaan under Joshua (*cf.* 11:29ff.; 27).

III. STIPULATIONS: COVENANT LIFE, 5:1-26:19

When suzerainty treaties were renewed, the stipulations, which constituted the long and crucial central section of the covenant, were repeated but with modifications, especially such as were necessary to meet the changing situation. So in these Deuteronomic stipulations Moses rehearses and reformulates the requirements promulgated in the Sinaitic Covenant. Furthermore, just as treaty stipulations customarily began with the fundamental and general demand for the vassal's absolute allegiance to the suzerain and then proceeded to various specific requirements, so Moses confronts Israel with the primary demand for consecration to Yahweh (chaps. 5-11) and then with the ancillary stipulations of covenant life (chaps. 12-26).

A. THE GREAT COMMANDMENT, 5:1-11:32

The covenant's first and great commandment, the requirement of perfect consecration to the Lord, is enunciated in chapters 5-7 and enforced by divine claims and sanctions in chapters 8-11. These subject divisions are not, however, rigid; the exhortative strand is pervasive. Analyzed in somewhat more detail, this section develops the theme of the great commandment as follows: Yahweh's existing covenantal claims upon Israel (chap. 5). The challenge of Yahweh's exclusive lordship over Israel, expressed as a principle (chap. 6) and a program (chap. 7). Warnings against the temptation to autonomy whether in the form of the spirit of self-sufficiency (chap. 8) or of self-righteousness (9:1-10:11). A call to true allegiance (10:12-11:32).

1. GOD'S COVENANT LORDSHIP, 5:1-33

5:1. *Hear . . . learn . . . keep . . . do.* This chapter opens and closes (vv. 32, 33) with a charge to follow carefully the divine stipulations of the covenant that was in process of solemnization.

5:2-5. *The Lord our God made a covenant with us in Horeb* (v. 2). The commitment to which Israel was summoned would be a renewal of the covenant relationship to Yahweh which already obtained. Forty years earlier at Sinai God had by covenant ceremony established Israel as his theocratic people

(v. 2). That was done in faithfulness to God's prior covenant promises to the patriarchs. *Not . . . with our fathers, but with us* (v. 3). The patriarchal *fathers* (v. 3; *cf.* 4:31, 37; 7:8, 12; 8:18) had died without receiving the promises; but the present generation, with whom the Sinaitic Covenant was established as well as with the older generation that perished in the wilderness (*cf.* 11:2), was privileged to see the promised kingdom realized (v. 3). *I stood between the Lord and you* (v. 5). At Sinai, as now, Moses was the mediator between God and Israel, an office the more needful because of Israel's fear of face to face confrontation with the fiery theophany (*cf.* 4:12). If the reporting role of Moses described parenthetically in verse 5 does not refer to revelations given after the promulgation of the Decalogue, then statements found elsewhere to the effect that Israel heard God declare the Decalogue (*e.g.*, 4:12; Ex. 19:9; 20:19) would mean that God's voice was audible but his words were indiscernible to Israel. However, verse 5 is more likely proleptic, like verse 22b.

5:6-22 [Heb. 5:6-18]. From the fact of the Sinaitic Covenant Moses proceeds to its documentary content as inscribed on the duplicate tables (*cf.* comments on 4:13). While continuing the thought that Israel was already covenantally bound to Yahweh, this achieves the additional purpose of incorporating the comprehensive summary of permanent covenant law into the stipulations section of the Deuteronomic renewal document. The Decalogue, being itself not simply a moral code but the text of a covenant, exhibits the treaty pattern as follows: preamble (v. 6a), historical prologue (v. 6b), and stipulations interspersed with curse and blessing formulae (vv. 7-21). (See further, Chapter 1 above.)

Keep the sabbath day to sanctify it (v. 12). Most significant of the variations from the form of the Decalogue as presented in Exodus 20:2-17 is the new formulation of the fourth word. The sabbatic cycle of covenant life symbolizes the consummation principle characteristic of divine action. God works, accomplishes his purpose and, rejoicing, rests. Exodus 20:11 refers to the exhibition of the consummation pattern in creation for the original model of the Sabbath; Deuteronomy 5:15 refers to its manifestation in redemption, where the divine triumph is such as to bring God's elect to their rest also. Most appropriately, therefore, was the Sabbath appointed as sign of God's covenant with the people he redeemed from the bondage of

Egypt to inherit the rest of Canaan (*cf*. Ex. 31:13-17). In keeping with the Deuteronomic interpretation of the Sabbath in terms of the progress of God's redemptive purpose is the New Testament's orientation of the Sabbath to the Saviour's resurrection triumph by which his redeemed people attain with him unto eternal rest. (For the possible use of the Sabbath law as Yahweh's treaty seal, see Chapter 1 above.)

Other notable Deuteronomic variations in the Decalogue are the reversal of the order of *wife* and *house* in the tenth word, and the addition there of *his field* (v. 21). The latter is added because Israel was about to enter upon a settled existence in the land, whereas during the wilderness wanderings such legislation would have been irrelevant. This is a good example of the kind of legislative modification found in secular renewal treaties.

These words the Lord spake . . . and he added no more (v. 22). The uniqueness of the revelation of the ten words is underscored in verse 22. That revelation alone was spoken directly by God to all Israel; it alone was written by God. It is the comprehensive summary of the law of God. More than that, it is the quintessence of the Mosaic administration of God's redemptive covenant.

5:23-27 [Heb. 5:20-24]. Continuing the account of the covenant making at Sinai, Moses reminded Israel of their former vow to obey God's voice (v. 27b; *cf*. Ex. 20:18-21). Indeed, such was their fear of God in the presence of his glory on the mount that they had desired Moses to receive the further revelations of the divine voice for them: *Go thou near, and hear . . . and speak thou unto us* (v. 27). Such reluctance to experience to the utmost of opportunity the presence of God is a far cry from man's original delight in communion with his Creator in the Garden. And therein is exposed the exceeding cursedness of the curse upon sin. There are of course ultimate limits to man's qualifications for the vision of God (*cf*. Ex. 33:20). But even though, within those limits, redemptive grace makes possible the enjoyment of a vision of God, fallen man regards the experience as a threat to his life (*cf*., *e.g.*, Gen. 32:30; Jud. 6:22, 23). In God's holy presence at Sinai the Israelites were so conscious of defilement that they feared to venture further with their unique privilege (vv. 25, 26; *cf*. 4:33). Nevertheless, their fear was godly for they acknowledged the God who appeared so terribly on Sinai as their God (*the Lord our God*, vv. 24, 25, 27) and committed themselves to do his will.

5:28-33 [Heb. 5:25-30]. What more stirring memories could Moses have evoked in anticipation of his concluding exhortation to walk in the way of the Lord and of life (vv. 32, 33) than those of God's approbation of Israel's previous vow (v. 28) and of his fatherly yearning that when the Sinaitic theophany should have ceased, the reverent devotion it had inspired might continue and thus it *might be well with them, and with their children forever* (v. 29). This account of the response of the Lord supplements the Exodus 20 record.

Chapters 6 and 7. In chapter 6 the principle of exclusive devotion to Yahweh is enunciated and with it the corollary prohibition of allegiance to alien deities. Then in chapter 7 the program of conquest is announced for the elimination of foreign gods and their people from the domain of Canaan, the land which was chosen by Yahweh as an earthly type of his eternal and universal kingdom.

2. THE PRINCIPLE OF CONSECRATION, 6:1-25

6:1-3. The commandments about to be given were the divinely dictated law for the theocratic kingdom as it was soon to be erected in the new paradise land of milk and honey. *Observe to do it; that it may be well with thee . . . as the Lord God of thy fathers hath promised thee* (v. 3). Israel's continued enjoyment of a habitation in God's land, like Adam's continued enjoyment of the original paradise, depended on continued fidelity to the Lord. Certain important distinctions are necessary in making such a comparison. Flawless obedience was the condition of Adam's continuance in the Garden; but Israel's tenure in Canaan was contingent on the maintenance of a measure of religious loyalty which needed not to be comprehensive of all Israel nor to be perfect even in those who were the true Israel. There was a freedom in God's exercise or restraint of judgment, a freedom originating in the underlying principle of sovereign grace in his rule over Israel. Nevertheless, God did so dispense his judgment that the interests of the typical-symbolical message of Israel's history were preserved. (See further the comments on chapters 27-30.)

6:4-9. *Yahweh is our God, Yahweh alone* (v. 4). This confession (various translations of which are grammatically possible) seems best understood as a practical equivalent or, more specifically, as a covenantal response to the revelation of monotheism (as recorded, for example, in 4:35 and 32:39; *cf.* 5:6, 7; I Chr. 29:1). "For though there be that are called gods, whether in heaven or in earth, (as there be gods many, and lords many,) but to us there is but one God, the Father . . . and one Lord Jesus Christ" (I Cor. 8:5, 6). Yahweh is unique; deity is confined to him exclusively. To Yahweh alone must Israel submit in religious covenant and him they must serve in the totality of their being with the intensity of love (v. 5). God's claim upon this exclusive and intensive devotion Jesus called the first and great commandment (Matt. 22:37, 38; Mark 12:29, 30; *cf.* Luke 10:25-28). It is the heart principle of all the covenant stipulations. The past mercies of God rehearsed in the historical prologue prompt such love and the love reveals itself in reverent obedience to all God's particular commandments (v. 6; *cf.* 11:1, 22; 19:9; 30:16; John 14:15). This passage is thus the text for all that follows. *Thou shalt teach them diligently unto thy children* (v. 7a). The family character of covenant administration requires that the children be brought under the government of the stipulations (*cf.* vv. 20ff.). Day and night the godly are to meditate on God's law (vv. 7b-9; *cf.* Ps. 1:2). In these verses Moses does not make ceremonial requirements but elaborates with concrete figures the demand for a constant focus of concern on the good pleasure of Israel's Lord. Verse 9 reflects architectural custom in the world of Moses' day. For the figurative use of such language, see Exodus 13:9, 16. A literal practice of the injunctions of verses 8, 9 came into vogue among later Jews in the form of the phylacteries worn on the person (*cf.* Matt. 23:5) and the mezuzah affixed over the doorpost.

6:10-19. The constant corollary of the demand for loyalty in ancient suzerainty treaties was the prohibition of allegiance to any and all other lords. So Yahweh forbade entanglement with the gods of Canaan: *Ye shall not go after other gods, of the gods of the people which are round about you* (v. 14). The temptation to such idolatry would be fierce since the claim made for the local Canaanite gods was that they were the bestowers of fertility and abundance in the land. *Beware lest thou forget the Lord* (v. 12). Such is human perversity that Israel, satisfied with the material plenty of a plundered culture, would be inclined to honor the vain claims of their victims' idols and to forget the claims of their own God who had saved from

Egypt and given victory in Canaan (vv. 10-12). *Thou shalt . . . swear by his name* (v. 13). Swearing by Yahweh's name was in effect a renewal of the oath of allegiance which ratified the covenant. It invoked God as the oath deity who avenged perfidy. *The Lord your God in the midst of you is a jealous God* (v. 15, RSV). The Lord was indeed present and jealously guarding the honor of his name taken in oath. Israel must not, therefore, presume to put God on trial, as at Massah (*cf.* Ex. 17:7), seeking proof of his presence and power to visit on them the covenant sanctions, whether blessing or curse. Let Israel rather be faithful and God would faithfully fulfill his good promises (vv. 17-19; *cf.* v. 10).

6:20-25. Seeing generations come and go had lengthened Moses' perspective. His interest was not confined to the present assembly but reached into the long future of God's kingdom (*cf.* v. 2). *When thy son asketh thee in time to come* (v. 20). Crucial to the well-being of the theocracy would be the faithful covenantal nurture of the children in the message of God's redemptive actions and purposes for his people. In particular, God's giving of the law furthered the purposes of mercy by revealing the path of righteousness, to follow which would lead to divine favor and blessing (v. 24). *It shall be our righteousness, if we observe to do all these commandments* (v. 25). Moses does not here present a works principle of salvation. The stress falls on the function of law as disclosing the standard of conduct which is righteous in God's sight and a love for which is a prerequisite for beatitude. It is the consistent teaching of Scripture that such righteousness comes bound up in the indivisible whole of salvation which is freely given by God in his grace through Jesus Christ.

3. THE PROGRAM OF CONQUEST, 7:1-26

7:1-5. In the Book of the Covenant produced at Sinai there was promulgated a program of conquest and extermination against the Canaanite people and cultus (*cf.* Ex. 23:20-33; 34:11-16). Thereby the ancient prophecy of Noah pronouncing Canaan accursed and the servant of Shem (Gen. 9:25, 26; *cf.* Gen. 10:15-18; Ex. 23:23) would be fulfilled (see, too, Gen. 15:16-21). The hour of divine judgment having now come, Moses charged Israel with the execution of that program. Everybody and everything in Canaan which was consecrated to idols rather than to the service of God must be consecrated to the wrath of God.

Seven nations (v. 1; *cf.* Josh. 3:10; 24:11); in such lists elsewhere the number varies from three to ten. The *seven* specified here possibly is a figure for completeness. *Thou shalt utterly destroy them; thou shalt make no covenant with them, nor show mercy unto them* (v. 2). The Hebrew root *ḥrm*, translated "utterly destroy" in the major English versions, means primarily "devote" and hence "ban" and "extirpate." Many have found a stumblingblock in this command to exterminate the Canaanites, as though it represented a sub-Christian ethic. Actually, the offense taken is taken at the theology and religion of the Bible as a whole. The New Testament, too, warns men of the realm of the everlasting ban where the reprobate, devoted to wrath, must magnify the justice of the God whom they have hated. The judgments of hell are the *ḥērem* principle come to full and final manifestation. Since the Old Testament theocracy in Canaan was a divinely appointed symbol of the consummate kingdom of God, there is found in connection with it an intrusive anticipation of the ethical pattern that will obtain at the final judgment and beyond. Moreover, the extermination of the Canaanites and the obliteration of their cultic installations, with their *altars, pillars, Asherim,* and *graven images* (v. 5, ASV), were necessary if Israel's calling to positive consecration to God in living service was to be fulfilled. For, because of Israel's frailty, the proximity of the Canaanites would lead to the dissolution of Israel's covenantal distinctiveness (v. 3), to foreign and idolatrous allegiances (v. 4a), and hence to Israel's own destruction (v. 4b). The program of conquest (chap. 7) is thus a consistent application of the principle of consecration (chap. 6; esp. 6:12-15).

7:6-16 For thou art an holy people unto the Lord thy God (v. 6). This was the goal of Israel's election that was to be promoted by the elimination of the Canaanites. The language of verse 6 recalls Exodus 19:5, 6, the classic formulation of the unique theocratic status for which Israel was chosen. *Not . . . because ye were more in number* (v. 7). High calling is attended by temptation to boasting (*cf.* Moses' concern with this problem in chaps. 8-10). Therefore, Israel was reminded to glory only in the name of God. In his sovereign love and faithfulness alone was to be found the explanation of Israel's election (v. 8; *cf.* 4:37), certainly not in Israel's size. For God chose their father Abraham, being only one, and the family of Jacob, which descended into Egypt as only some seventy souls (v. 7; cf. 10:22). It followed from the sovereignty of God's grace that Israel had no claims upon him that might encourage carelessness with respect to his covenant demands and sanctions. *He will not be slack to him that hateth him* (v. 10). Alluding to the sanction formulae which were affixed to the second commandment, Moses encouraged obedience (v. 11) by declaring that though unmerited grace would be continued to the thousandth generation (v. 9; cf. 5:10), apostate despisers of grace and holiness would discover the covenant curses were no idle threats (vv. 9-11). Similarly, the faithful might be confident that the covenant blessings were no empty promises: *The Lord thy God shall keep unto thee the covenant and the mercy which he sware unto thy fathers* (v. 12; cf. Gen. 12:2, 3; Ex. 23:22-31). Yahweh the Creator, not Baal, was the bestower of fertility in field, flock, and family (vv. 13, 14). It was the Lord who had subjected man to nature's curse for his sin and he was able therefore to deliver the Israelites from the curse of Egypt's notorious diseases (*e.g.,* elephantiasis, dysentery, and ophthalmia), just as he had rescued them from Egypt's infamous pharaoh (v. 15; cf. v. 8; Ex. 15:26). Verse 16 summarizes, repeating the programmatic command and its purpose.

7:17-26. *How can I dispossess them* (v. 17)? Though in respect to the privileges of election Israel was tempted to vanity, in the face of the responsibility of their commission they were tempted to timidity (v. 17; cf. Num. 13:31ff.). In answer to any such rising fears Moses reminded them of that wondrous experience in Egypt during their youth when by mighty signs their God saved them (vv. 18, 19a). *The Lord thy God is among you, a mighty God and terrible* (v. 21). He assured them that this same terrible God was still in their midst to war in their behalf against the Canaanite kings (vv. 19b-24). Whom then should they fear? *The hornet* (v. 20; cf. Ex. 23:28; Josh. 24:12) is not here a symbol for pharaoh's power though it be so in Egyptian usage. It is rather a figure for the terror of God which, descending on Israel's foes, produced panic and rout (*cf.* v. 23). The fact that certain species of hornet in Palestine build nests underground and in rock crevices suggests the appropriateness of the figure to the destruction of Canaanites in hiding. Some would translate the Hebrew word not "hornet" but "discouragement." *Little by little* (v. 22); cf. Exodus 23:29,

30; Judges 2:20-23; 3:1, 2. God's gradual dispossessing of the Canaanites, designed for Israel's good, was suspended after Israel's post-Joshuan apostasy as a chastisement. *Lest thou be snared therein . . . and be a cursed thing like it* (vv. 25, 26). Reassuring promise turns into renewed warning and imperative (*cf.* v. 5). To appropriate that which had fallen under God's ban would be to forfeit the status of covenant favor and place oneself under the divine anathema (*cf.* Josh. 7).

Chapters 8-11. Absolute allegiance to Yahweh as Lord (6:4ff.) meant that the Israelites must refrain from simultaneous service to any other god-king (6:12ff.; 7:1ff.), but it also meant that they might not declare their religious independence. Moses therefore enforced the fundamental obligation of whole-souled devotion to God by warning against the dangers of an autonomous attitude, whether manifested in the spirit of self-sufficiency (chap. 8) or the spirit of self-righteousness (9:1-10:11). These negative warnings having been issued, Moses concluded this section with a positive challenge to submit to Yahweh's lordship (10:12-11:32).

4. THE LAW OF THE MANNA, 8:1-20

The focal point of this chapter is verse 17 with its picture of a future Israel at ease in Canaan, basking in self-congratulations. The recollection of God's providential guidance during the forty years in the wilderness (vv. 2ff.) would afford the corrective for such vanity.

8:1-6. Verse 1 is another introductory summary of the covenant summons and sanctions (see also 4:1; 5:1; 6:1). *Thou shalt remember all the way which the Lord thy God led thee these forty years in the wilderness* (v. 2). So far as the surviving generation was concerned, the wilderness experience was designed for probationary (v. 2b; *cf.* 13:3) and propaedeutic (v. 3b) purposes. *As a man chasteneth his son* (v. 5). It was a fatherly discipline and contributed to their ultimate blessing (*cf.* v. 16b). *He fed thee with manna, which thou knewest not* (v. 3). What is meant by God's humbling Israel (v. 2) is illustrated by reference to God's extraordinary provision for every need during the forty years (vv. 3, 4; *cf.* 29:5, 6), particularly by means of the manna (*cf.* Ex. 16, esp. v. 4). Humbling consisted of privation and then the provision of the "What-is-it?" the unknown, supernatural bread of heaven, which compelled them to recognize their dependence on God (*cf.* v. 16a). Whatever substrative role was or was not played by the honey-like excretions of scale-insects found in tamarisk thickets in the Sinai area and identified by modern naturalistic exegesis as the biblical manna, the bread of heaven was none the less in its nature and manner of provision clearly a miraculous product. Moreover, a mere change from one normal, palatable food staple to another, no matter how exotic, would neither have humbled Israel nor taught them the truth which the manna did: *Man doth not live by bread alone but by every word that proceedeth out of the mouth of the Lord doth man live* (v. 3b, ASV).

As an effective reminder that the creature does not exist as a self-sufficient being, sustained by the fruits of an earth also existing and producing independently of God, but as one ultimately and always dependent on the divine word which called him and his world into being, God led Israel into a situation where life was derived and must be daily sought from a heavenly bread, the fruit of a daily creative exercise of the word of God. And that they might see that man's life does not, as does the life of a beast, consist solely in a physical vitality which bread, whether earthly or heavenly, might sustain, God provided the bread of heaven in such a way as to require an ethical-religious response to his preceptive word. This response was appropriately focused on the observance of the Sabbath, the sign of man's covenant allegiance, as well as the recaller of God's role as Creator. The manna thus taught Israel that only as man stands obediently under his Lord's sovereign word (v. 6), the ultimate source of life, does he find true and lasting life (*cf.* 30:20). For Moses, the way to true life included dying by the power as well as according to the direction of that sovereign word (34:5). So it was also with Christ (Matt. 4:4; cf. John 10:18).

8:7-20. *For the Lord thy God bringeth thee into a good land* (v. 7). The recollection of the wilderness lesson was necessary at this particular juncture, for God was about to conduct Israel into a land where the normal products of nature would afford a comparatively luxurious standard of living (vv. 7-9). *A land whose stones are iron* (v. 9). In the sandstone substratum of Palestine are copper and iron veins, and ancient mining operations have been discovered where this sandstone outcrops in the Arabah. Though all these natural products should be gratefully recognized as the gifts of God just as much as the supernatural manna (v. 10b), luxury and ease (vv. 12, 13) would blunt the edge of Israel's awareness of God (v. 11). Pride would suppress the memory of humbler days of slavery, scorpions, and thirst, days when deliverance and survival required divine intervention by hitherto unknown ways (vv. 14-16). *My power and the might of mine hand hath gotten me this wealth* (v. 17). Of such denial of their Lord through self-adulation they must beware. The same truth that had to be learned in the former days of empty stomachs would be the relevant truth in the coming days of full stomachs: the source of man's life is the word of God (v. 18a). All Israel's beatitude would be attributable solely to God's fidelity to his covenant oath (v. 18b; *cf.* Gen. 15). At the same time the Lord as the God of Israel's self-maledictory oath of allegiance would with equal fidelity visit upon covenant-breakers the curses which they had invoked: *If thou do at all forget the Lord . . . ye shall surely perish* (v. 19). Repudiation of election as Yahweh's peculiar possession and identification with the anathematized Canaanites in their idolatrous iniquity would result in Israel's identification with them in their doom (v. 20).

5. THE WARNING OF THE BROKEN TABLETS, 9:1-10:11

For Israel to assume that Canaan was a reward for their righteousness (9:4) would be an even greater contradiction of the realities of the covenant relationship than their boasting that the possession and prosperity of the land were an achievement of their might (8:17). The conceit of self-righteousness is an attempt of the sinner lusting after autonomy to free himself from God at that very point where his need of God is most desperate — the need for forgiveness and cleansing. Moses therefore passionately presented the truth that the promises and blessings of the covenant relation were Israel's by virtue of mercy, not of merit.

9:1-5. *Understand therefore this day, that the Lord thy God is he which goeth over before thee* (v. 3). The occasion for this admonition was the imminent prospect of Israel's dispossessing a people reputedly invincible in offensive combat and defended by seemingly impregnable fortifications, rising like the tower of Babel up to the heaven (vv. 1, 2). *Who can stand before the children of Anak* (v. 2)? On the Anakim and other impressive people, see 1:28; 4:38; 7:1; Num. 13:28. The spearhead of Israel's advance, however, was the One who dwelt in the heavens and made the highest mountains of earth his footstool, who was moreover a devouring fire (*cf.* 4:24; 7:17ff.). *Speak not thou in thine heart, . . . saying, For my righteousness the Lord hath brought me in to possess this land* (v. 4). This was the tragic misinterpretation of the conquest events to which Israel would be prone in defiance of all the obvious historic facts and God's explicit warning to the contrary. The explanation of Israel's triumph could lie only in the wickedness of the Canaanites on the one side (vv. 4b, 5) and in God's forgiving grace to Israel on the other (9:6-10:11). For the relationship of the iniquity of the inhabitants of Canaan to the fulfillment of the promises of the Abrahamic Covenant, see Genesis 15:16. Archaeological investigation has revealed the abysmal depths of moral degeneration in Canaanite society and religion in the Mosaic age. The way in which Israel's acquisition of their promised land was bound up with the elimination of the Canaanites exemplifies the principle of redemptive judgment. The salvation of the friends of God necessarily involves their triumph over the friends of Satan. The judgment of the latter is, from the viewpoint of the elect, a redemptive intervention of God. See, for example, the prophetic visions of Revelation 19:11ff. and 20:9, in which it is by the doom of the satanic hordes that the redemption of the elect is consummated.

9:6-10:11. Israel's self-righteous interpretation of the conquest had been contradicted in advance by all Moses' experience with them during the forty years past (9:7, 24). They had repeatedly shown themselves to be a fractious, covenant-breaking people (9:6-17, 21-24). They had been spared and preserved in covenant relationship to God only through God's merciful renewal of the broken covenant (10:1-11) in response to the importunate mediatorial intercession of Moses (9:18-20, 25-29).

Also in Horeb ye provoked the Lord to wrath (9:8). The classic example of Israel's faithlessness occurred at the very time that the covenant was being solemnized at Horeb (9:8ff.; *cf.* Ex. 32). Israel had just sworn allegiance to God and vowed obedience to his commandments (Ex. 24). Indeed, it was while the Lord was in the very process of inscribing the treaty on the duplicate stone documents during Moses' first stay of forty days and nights on the mount that Israel broke the covenant by engaging in idolatry (9:9-12). In that hour the wrath of God blazed and Israel was at the brink of destruction: *Let me alone, that I may destroy them, and blot out their name from under heaven* (9:14; *cf.* v. 19a). So far as merit was concerned, therefore, Israel deserved not to inherit the bounties of Canaan but to fall under the ban along with the dispossessed Canaanites. *I took the two tables . . . and break them before your eyes* (9:17). Moses' treatment of the treaty tablets and the golden calf (9:21) was symbolic of the shattering of the covenant. Such ritual procedure is attested in ancient state treaties in connection with a vassal's violation of his oath. (See further above, p. 43). *And at Taberah, and at Massah, and at Kibroth-hattaavah* (9:22). Other instances of Israel's provoking God's wrath preceded (9:7) and followed the day of assembly at Sinai (9:22; *cf.* Ex. 17:2-7; Num. 11) until their perversity at Kadesh-barnea (9:23; *cf.* 1:26ff.; Num. 13, 14) brought the verdict of exile unto death upon the older generation.

I fell down before the Lord . . . the Lord hearkened unto me at that time also (9:18, 19). More than once the ultimate doom of the covenant curses had been averted through the intercession of Moses (9:18-20, 25-29). In this more remarkably than in any other aspect of his ministry Moses' mediatorship prefigured the antitypical mediatorship of Christ, who also "made intercession for the transgressors" (Isa. 53:12). When at Sinai God threatened to blot out Israel and offered to exalt Moses' descendants as a new covenant nation (9:14; *cf.* Ex. 32:10), Moses faithfully fulfilled his mediatorial office in behalf of Israel rather than grasp at the opportunity to be a second Abraham. In fact, he offered himself as a second Isaac on the altar. If there must be a blotting out, Moses pleaded that rather than being the one exception to the judgment he alone might be blotted out as a means of securing forgiveness for the others (*cf.* Ex. 32:32). He "stood before him in the breach to turn away his wrath lest he should destroy them" (Ps. 106:23).

The intercession referred to in Deuteronomy 9:18, 19, 25-29 (*cf.* 10:10) was offered during Moses' second forty days on the mount. Difficulty has been found in the fact that the content of Moses' prayer (9:26-29) corresponds to that recorded in Exodus 32:11-13, for it has been assumed that the latter refers to Moses' first forty days before God. Actually, Exodus 32:11-14 is an introductory summation of the following account, which embraces the second period of forty days. The immediate chronological sequence is from Exodus 32:10 to 32:15, as is reflected in Deuteronomy 9:14, 15. The Exodus narrative from 32:30-34:29 possibly all refers to the second forty days and their sequel, not to preceding events; the arrangement, as often in Hebrew narrative (*cf.* Deut. 9 itself), subordinates strict chronological sequence to topical interests. For "at that time also" (9:19; 10:10), "even at that time" would be better, giving *gam* its more frequent emphatic sense.

The Lord was very angry with Aaron to have destroyed him (9:20). God's particular wrath against Aaron, not mentioned in the Exodus account, is cited here to demonstrate how completely devoid of merit and dependent on mercy Israel was — even their highpriest was a brand plucked from the burning! The same truth is apparent from the grounds of Moses' intercession (9:26-29). He pleaded for a stay of judgment in spite of Israel's stubborn wickedness (v. 27b) and only on the basis of God's interest in his own name among the nations of the earth. *Lest the land whence thou broughtest us out say, Because the Lord was not able* (9:28). God had from of old declared his sovereign purposes of redemptive judgment (cf. v. 27a) and had identified that program with his dealings with Israel and Egypt (v.26). If now he destroyed Israel, even though he would not thus violate his covenant and though he would still faithfully fulfill his promises to the patriarchs through Mosaic descendants (*cf.* 9:14), such a procedure would be liable to misunderstanding. The significance of God's mighty revelation of his name in judgment and salvation at the exodus would be obscured and the fear of him diminished by contempt for what would be misinterpreted as weakness.

The renewal of the covenant (10:1-11) after Israel's idolatry at Sinai was, therefore, due solely to divine grace. *Hew thee two tables of stone like unto the first* (v. 1). Part of the ceremony of renewal was the preparation of the two new treaty tablets. See Exodus 34:1-4a, which possibly belongs chronologically between 32:29 and 32:30. Similarly, Deuteronomy 10:1a precedes in time 9:18ff. and 9:25ff. There is further disregard for chronological distinctions within 10:1-5, for the construction of the ark as the depository for the stone tablets is interwoven with the account of the hewing and engraving of this second set of treaty texts. It was actually after the second period of forty days that Moses had Bezaleel construct the ark (Ex. 35:30ff.; 36:2; 37:1), and it was of course still later that Moses put the testimony in the ark (Ex. 40:20) and then put the ark in the tabernacle (Ex. 40:21). The condensed, summarizing treatment in Deuteronomy 10:1-5 reflects the requirement found in the international suzerainty treaties that the duplicate covenant texts were to be deposited in the sanctuaries of the two covenant parties in order thus to be under the surveillance of the oath deities. In the case of God's covenant with Israel there was but one sanctuary involved since God, the covenant Suzerain, was also the God who had his sanctuary in Israel. (See further above, p. 19). The purpose of 10:1-5 being to state in a comprehensive and general way that God had mercifully re-confirmed the covenant with the rebellious vassals, Moses included the matter of the ark as a familiar and integral element in the standard ratification procedure.

Deuteronomy 10:6, 7, with which verses 8 and 9 belong materially, constitutes a stylistic break. It is uncertain whether this excursus originated as a quotation read from an itinerary in the course of Moses' address, whether he parenthetically inserted it when writing the Book of the Law, or whether someone like the author of Deuteronomy 34 added it. *The children of Israel took their journey* (v. 6a). The journey in view (vv. 6, 7) is that southward from Kadesh recorded in Numbers 33:37; for the particular stations, see Numbers 33:30-33. *Eleazer his son ministered in the priest's office in his stead* (v. 6b). These verses are relevant to the context, for they further enhance the covenant renewing grace of God by recalling that God re-instituted the priesthood of Aaron of the tribe of Levi and continued it in Aaron's son Eleazer in spite of his anger against the father (9:20). This thought is supplemented by the mention of the separation of the entire tribe of Levi to its ministry of blessing in Israel (10:8, 9; *cf.* Ex. 28 and 29; Num. 1:49ff.; 3:9ff.; 4:17ff.; 8:6ff.; 18:20-24). In part, the particular functions listed were performed by the Levite tribe through its priestly-Aaronic family. The intercession theme (*cf.* 9:18ff.) is concluded in 10:10, 11. *The land, which I sware unto their fathers to give unto them* (v. 11). The journey to the promised homeland of which Israel was so utterly undeserving was to be resumed because of God's regard for his own name, the name he had taken in oath because he could swear by no higher (*cf.* Ex. 33:1ff.).

6. A CALL TO COMMITMENT, 10:12-11:32

Israel was confronted with the great covenantal decision, the choice between the blessing and the curse (11:26-32). Moses enforced the call to obedience (10:12ff.; 11:1, 8, 13, 18ff., 32) by focusing the eyes of the people on him who addressed to them his covenant as the righteous Judge of heaven and earth (10:12-22), whose impartial judgment Israel had in the past seen irresistibly executed in Egypt and in the wilderness (11:1-7) and should in the future find sovereignly exercised over the land and inhabitants of Canaan (11:8-25).

10:12-22. *And now* (v. 12a); this introduces the conclusion to a major division of the address (*cf.* 4:1). *What doth the Lord thy God require of thee* (v. 12)? The basic and comprehensive covenant requirement is here repeated (vv. 12, 13, 20; *cf.* 6:5, 13, 24; Mic. 6:8). True fear and true love are complementary and inseparable. They are the response of a true heart to God's majesty and goodness, respectively, and together they are productive of wholehearted service in obedience to all God's good pleasure. *Circumcise . . . your heart* (v. 16). Genuine devotion can flow only from a heart that has experienced the reality of that qualification which was symbolized in the initiatory sign of the covenant (*cf.* 30:6; Ex. 6:12, 30; Lev. 26:41; Jer. 6:10; 9:25, 26). *He is thy praise, and he is thy God* (v. 21). To inspire the fear of Yahweh, Moses summoned Israel to behold him as Lord of the cosmos (v. 14), as God above all that be called gods (v. 17a), as righteous Judge (v. 17b), and as Sovereign over history and nature (v. 21). To encourage love toward him, Moses recalled how God had bestowed the privilege of covenant status on Israel's ancestors (v. 15a), fulfilled the patriarchal promises (vv. 15b, 21, 22), and shown himself a Helper of the helpless (vv. 18, 19).

11:1-7. The charge to love Yahweh (v. 1) is a connecting refrain in 10:12-11:32. After *And know ye this day* (v. 2), there is a parenthetical remark (see RSV), which notes that the summons to covenantal decision was not addressed to the children born in the wilderness. It was rather directed to those who had been born in Egypt and had seen God's great acts of judgment in the past (v. 7). The object of *know ye* (v. 2) is *the discipline of the Lord your God, his greatness, etc.* (vv. 2ff., RSV). Israel had been disciplined to reverence the Lord as the Judge with whom they had to do by their experience of his judgment on their enemies (vv. 2-4) and themselves alike (vv. 5, 6). They knew, therefore, that his judgment was almighty, so that the mightiest on earth could not prevent it, and it was impartially righteous, so that even his covenant people dared not presume upon their election. On 11:6, *cf.* Numbers 16, especially vv. 31-33. Moses' silence here with respect to the rebel Korah was possibly in deference to the surviving Levitical Korahites (cf. Num. 26:11).

11:8-25. From Israel's future, too, Moses adduced motives for obedience. *That ye may go in and possess the land . . . and that ye may prolong your days in the land* (vv. 8, 9). On the relation of Israel's tenure on the land to her covenant fidelity, see comments on 6:1-3. *A land which the Lord thy God careth for* (v. 12). Unlike Egypt with its irrigation agriculture (v. 10), Canaan was clearly dependent for its fruitfulness on the direct blessing of God (vv. 11, 12; cf. 8:7ff.). And in that sphere God's righteous judgment with respect to Israel's conduct would be registered (vv. 13-17). *The rain of your land in its season* (v. 14, ASV). Prosperity would depend on proper weather conditions the year around, especially important being the timely commencement of the rainy season in the fall and the due extension of the latter rains in the spring (v. 14). The very state of nature would thus constantly serve as a sensitive barometer of Israel's standing before the Lord. Therefore, Israel must be on guard against the spiritual dangers of material abundance (vv. 14b-16). For bounty can turn into drought, famine, and death at the mere word of Yahweh, the impartial, almighty Judge at whose command even the earth opened its mouth to swallow the Israelites Dathan and Abiram (v. 17; cf. 11:6; 6:11-15; 8:11-20).

Lay up these words in your heart (v. 18). On verses 18-20, cf. 6:6-9. Covenant loyalty from generation to generation would result in the perpetuation of Israel's possession of the promised land *as the days of heaven upon the earth* (v. 21), *i.e.*, as long as the heavens continue above the earth, in short, forever (cf. Ps. 72:5, 7, 17; 89:29). By the same token, infidelity must lead to termination of tenure. Success in the stipulated program of conquest (vv. 23-25; cf. 7:1f., 17ff.; 9:1ff.) would depend first and last not on military prowess but on religious commitment (v. 22). For the nations as well as nature (cf. vv. 8-17) were under Yahweh's absolute control. Fulfillment of the great commandment to love the Lord would be blessed with inheritance of the land of promise to its utmost boundaries: from the wilderness of the Sinai peninsula on the south to the Lebanon mountains on the north and from the Euphrates on the east to the Mediterranean on the west (v. 24; cf. 1:7; Gen. 15:18).

11:26-32. *A blessing and a curse* (v. 26). Here is the sum and conclusion of the whole matter (vv. 26-28). The lordship of

Yahweh declared in the covenant now being renewed unto Israel could be manifested in either blessing or curse (*cf.* Deut. 28; 30:15-20). The decision was Israel's. This twofold prospect and its challenge which Moses placed before Israel this day in Moab would be set before them again by Joshua on the other side of the Jordan in Canaan, that Israel might be careful to obey God and live (vv. 29-32). The transition from the Mosaic to Joshuan leadership was thus to be marked by a two-stage renewal ritual which exhibited the continuity of the more ultimate divine leadership. This arrangement was the equivalent of measures taken in vassal treaties by human suzerains to guarantee the dynastic succession on their thrones. (See further above, p. 36). See Deuteronomy 27 for the more detailed directions concerning the second stage of the ceremony to be conducted on Mount Gerizim and Mount Ebal (*cf.* Josh. 8:30-35).

B. ANCILLARY COMMANDMENTS, 12:1-26:19

Having delineated the inner spirit of theocratic life (chaps. 5-11), Moses goes on to detail the ordinances and institutions of the theocracy's outward form (chaps. 12-26). Chapters 12:1-16:17 are primarily concerned with cultic-ceremonial consecration requirements. Governmental and judicial authority is the subject in 16:18-21:23. The sphere of the mutual relationships of the theocratic citizens is covered by the legislation in 22:1-25:19. The stipulations conclude with rituals of cultic confession of Yahweh's lordship and a final declaration of covenant ratification (chap. 26).

1. CULTIC-CEREMONIAL CONSECRATION, 12:1-16:17

The central interest of the laws of this section is to guarantee a thoroughgoing consecration to Yahweh. Governing all the demands for tributary service in tithe (14:22ff.), first-fruits (15:19ff.), and sacrificial offerings (16:1ff.) is the law of the central altar with which this section opens (chap. 12). Singleness of devotion to the Lord was safeguarded by the imposition of the severest penalties on all who enticed to or became guilty of apostasy (chap. 13).

a. ALLEGIANCE TO GOD'S ALTAR, 12:1-32

12:1-3. *In the land* (v. 1; *cf.* 6:1). In the prophetic perspective of the following stipulations Israel is viewed as already in possession of their inheritance. *Ye shall utterly destroy all the places,*

wherein the nations which ye shall possess served their gods
(v. 2). This section connects with the preceding by resuming
that part of the mandate of conquest which required the obliteration of Canaanite cultic centers and installations (vv. 2, 3; *cf.*
7:5, 25; Ex. 23:24; 34:13). The execution of the program of
conquest as a whole would bring the tribes into control of
idolatrous shrines throughout the land (*cf.* Isa. 1:29; 57:5; 65:7;
Jer. 2:20; 3:6; 17:2; Ezek. 66:13; 18:6ff.; Hos. 4:13; I Kgs. 14:23;
II Kgs. 16:4; 17:10) and these would present a temptation to
religious syncretism (vv. 29, 30). The Israelites would be in
danger of adopting abominations like the fiery votive offering
of children (v. 31; *cf.* 18:10; Lev. 18:21; II Kgs. 16:3; 17:17;
21:6; 23:10; Jer. 7:31; 19:5; 32:35). In addition to the punitive
purpose of the destruction of Canaanite cultic sites there was
therefore the preventive design of protecting Israel against en-
snarement in the Canaanite cultic rites. The fact that the law
of the central sanctuary (vv. 4ff.) is thus introduced (vv. 2, 3)
and concluded (vv. 29-31) by such references to the Canaanite
cultus shows that one purpose of the centralization of Israelite
worship, too, was to avoid the contamination of the pure worship
of Yahweh by idolatrous practices.

The centralization requirement must also be understood in
terms of Deuteronomy's nature as a suzerainty treaty. Such
treaties prohibited the vassal to engage in any independent
diplomacy with a foreign power other than the covenant suzerain.
In particular, the vassal must not pay tribute to any other lord.
Similarly, all the requirements and prohibitions of Deuteronomy
12 were calculated to secure for Yahweh all Israel's tributary
sacrifice and offering. Israel must not pay any sacrificial tribute
to other gods, for such an impossible attempt to serve two
masters would be rebellion against the great commandment of
Yahweh's covenant.

In the promised land, the law of the central altar would
involve both the centralization of the special sacrificial festivals
(vv. 4-14) and the decentralization of the common family feasts
(vv. 15-28).

12:4-14. In contrast to the multiplicity of altars among the
Canaanites (v. 4), who sacrificed wherever they pleased (*cf.*
v. 13), Israel was to have one central altar and that at *the place
which the Lord your God shall choose* (v. 5). This oneness of
the sanctuary corresponded to the oneness of the divine lordship
over Israel (*cf.* 6:4,5).

Modern higher criticism has erroneously held that the concept of the central altar taught in Deuteronomy (or according to some, only in Deut. 12:1-7, which is then regarded as a later interpolation) stands in contradiction to other biblical legislation (*cf.*, especially, in the Book of the Covenant, Ex. 20:24). The Deuteronomic requirement has therefore been judged to be a later modification of earlier, supposedly laxer practice. The book as a whole has been dated in the 7th century B.C. and identified as the law book found in Josiah's day. A more recent approach of critics is to resolve the supposed conflict of codes not by placing them in a chronological sequence across the centuries, but by assigning to each a different geographic-cultic provenance. Deuteronomy is thought to represent the northern, Levitical outlook, the central sanctuary in view being Shechem. Some critics have even allowed that the centralization law in Deuteronomy might represent a return to an earlier, pre-monarchical ideal of the amphictyony.

Actually the Deuteronomic law of the altar represented no radical departure from previous legislation on this subject. In fact, Deuteronomy confirmed the fundamental principle formulated in the Sinaitic Book of the Covenant according to which altars were authorized only at places where God recorded his name, that is, at places of special divine revelation, particularly theophany (see Ex. 20:24 and compare Deut. 12:5a and 11). This relationship between altar and theophany is a constant element, but it also accounts for the emergence of minor modifications. For significant changes in the nature of theophany from era to era required corresponding changes with respect to the altar. Thus, during the days of the patriarchs altars were frequently erected at the various sites where God appeared, but there was not a continuing central altar until there was a continuing revelation of the presence of God in the form of the Shekinah glory tabernacling in the midst of Israel. This form of theophany began in the Mosaic era and the covenant stipulations given at Sinai, though they did not exclude altars at other places where God might record his name, were concerned primarily with the continuing central or official altar which would be associated with this abiding Shekinah theophany.

Another significant development in the history of theophany was envisaged in the Deuteronomic stipulations. During the wilderness wanderings of Israel the Shekinah moved from one location to another, and the central altar with it. But the day was coming when the Lord would choose a permanent place of habitation for his name within the promised land and that would require that the central altar become stationary too. Deuteronomy provides for this permanent establishment of the central altar at the site God would choose and that provision (not the centralization of the altar as such) is what is new in the Deuteronomic law of the altar. *When he giveth you rest from all your enemies round about, so that ye dwell in safety* (v. 10). Even the new circumstances of a permanent location must await the attainment of peace and rest (*cf.* Heb. 4:1ff.), a condition which fully arrived at the Old Testament typical level only in the days of David and Solomon (II Sam. 7:1; I Kgs. 5:4). Only then did God choose out of all the tribes the city of Jerusalem as the site for his house (I Kgs. 8:16, 44, 48; 11:13, 32, 36; 14:21; II Kgs. 21:7; 23:27), though at the first he had recorded his name temporarily at Shiloh (Jer. 7:12; Jud. 21:19). Furthermore, the Mosaic law of the central altar, while regulating the prescribed and ordinary sacrificial service of Israel (vv. 6, 7, 11ff.) as it was to be performed particularly at the three principal festivals of Passover, Pentecost, and Tabernacles, also recognized the possibility of revelatory action of God apart from the central altar and allowed for the specially appointed service and altar (*cf.* 27:5ff.). The accent thus falls more heavily on the purity than the unity of the cultus.

Also prominent in Moses' thought of covenant communion with the Lord was the note of joy: *Ye shall rejoice before the Lord your God* (v. 12; cf. v. 7). Love to God expressed in joyful worship was also to find its corollary in love to the brethren, especially in kindness to those, like the Levites (v. 12; *cf.* v. 19), who were dependent on the generosity, or indeed on the piety, of the congregation (*cf.* Num. 18:21; 35:1ff.). Contrasting the future arrangements to present practice Moses says that even under his leadership each Israelite was doing whatever was *right in his own eyes* (v. 8; *cf.* Judg. 17:6; 21:25). Here at least this expression is not derogatory; it apparently describes liberty, not license. Specifically, it indicates that there was no need to reckon as yet with distinctions such as that between sacrificial feasts (vv. 4-14) and family feasts (vv. 15-28).

12:15-28. *Notwithstanding thou mayest kill and eat flesh in*

all thy gates (v. 15). Besides bringing the Israelite tribes into
contact with heathen shrines, the inheriting of Canaan would
locate the tribal homes at considerable distances from Israel's
own central sanctuary (v. 21). If the stipulations of verses
4-14 were to be carried out in that new situation, a distinction
had to be made between the slaughtering and eating of animals
suitable for sacrifice as a sacrificial feast and the use of them
in an ordinary meal, and permission must be granted for the
decentralization of the latter. This new provision constituted
a modification of the requirements of Leviticus 17:1ff., which
governed the Israelites' consumption of flesh while they were
a compact camp about the tabernacle in the wilderness. *The
unclean and the clean may eat of it as of the gazelle and as of
the hart* (v. 15b, RSV; *cf.* v. 22). Participation in the family
feast was not dependent on ceremonial condition (*cf.* Lev.
7:19ff.) and the kind of meat permissible included that which
was proper for sacrifice as well as meat like game (*cf.* 14:5),
which was not sacrificially acceptable.

Attached to this permission were certain restrictions. One
was the familiar prohibition of blood (vv. 16, 23ff.; *cf.* Lev.
17:10ff.; Gen. 9:4). *Ye shall pour it upon the earth as water* (v.
16b). Pouring the blood upon the ground would be a safeguard
against pouring it as a sacrifice on some nearby, illegally remaining Canaanite altar. The centralization of the slaughter of all
animals fit for sacrifice during the wilderness journeyings was
explicitly designed to avoid such temptation (*cf.* Lev. 17:7).
Thou mayest not eat within thy gates the tithe (v. 17). Another
proviso or better a clarification of the permission of verse 15
was the reminder that all holy gifts to the Lord must be taken
to the place of the central sanctuary which God should choose
(vv. 17f., 26f.). That is, the permission operates within the
positive requirements of verses 4-14 (*cf.* esp. vv. 6, 11). *Thou
shalt not eat it; that it may go well with thee* (v. 25). The
interspersing of exhortation among the stipulations (vv. 25,
28) is one of the identifying marks of the Deuteronomic legislation as treaty stipulations rather than as a legal code.

12:29-32. On verses 29-31, see comments on verses 1-3. *Thou
shalt not add thereto, nor diminish from it* (v. 32; 13:1 in
Hebrew). Repeating essentially 4:2, Moses again declares that
the only true standard of ethics and godly service is the revealed will of God, no less, no more.

). RESISTANCE TO APOSTASY, 13:1-18

:nt suzerainty treaties it was required of the
...ι ne must not connive at evil words spoken against the
ʒuzerain, whether they amounted to an affront or to a conspiracy.
The vassal must report the insult or the fomenting of revolt.
In case of active rebellion he must undertake military measures
against the offenders. Moreover, he must manifest fidelity to his
lord in such cases no matter who the rebel might be, whether
prince or nearest relative. All of this finds its formal counterpart
in Deuteronomy 13. Stylistically, it is cast in the casuistic form
characteristic of ancient law codes but also of some treaty stipulations. Three cases of rebellion against Yahweh are dealt with.
The first two relate to the instigation stage, the guilty parties
being sign-attested claimants to revelation (vv. 1-5) and the
vassal's nearest relative or companion (vv. 6-11). The third
case concerns a city that has succumbed to enticement to rebel
against Yahweh and has become guilty of serving idol-lords
(vv. 12-18).

13:1-5 [Heb. 13:2-6]. *A prophet or a dreamer of dreams*
(v. 1). Intimation of the prophetic institution to be established
in Israel had already been given. God's self-disclosure to the
prophets would be through the media of vision and dream (Num.
12:5; *cf.* Deut. 18:15ff.). Even if one with impressive credentials
to the effect that he was a channel of revelation (vv. 1b, 2a)
should incite Israel to render allegiance and tribute to other
gods (v. 2b; *cf.* vv. 3b, 5b), his counsel must be despised (v.
3a; *cf.* Gal. 1:8, 9). *Sign or a wonder* (vv. 1, 2); both terms
can refer to an event which is in itself either ordinary or extraordinary. Here they apparently refer to a predicted event, not
necessarily miraculous, which coming to pass is claimed as a
sign of genuine prophetic vocation and authority. *Saying* (v. 2)
is to be taken with *if there arise among you a prophet* (v. 1).
Israel's standard of life and worship was God's covenant revelation through Moses, spoken and inscripturated; the fundamental
demand thereof was exclusive allegiance to Yahweh (v. 4).
*The Lord your God proveth you, to know whether ye love the
Lord your God* (v. 3b). It was in order to test Israel's obedience
to that paramount stipulation that God would permit the false
prophet to arise. *That prophet, or that dreamer of dreams,
shall be put to death* (v. 5). It was because their counsel was
to repudiate Yahweh's demand for loyalty, the very essence of
the covenant (*cf.* 6:4, 5; Ex. 20:3), that the ultimate penalty

was prescribed for them. Notice the quotations from the preamble and historical prologue of the covenant tablets (*cf.* Ex. 20:2). The execution of the instigator to defection would *burn out* the evil from the midst of Israel which, if it remained and spread, would result in the burning out of many in Israel (*cf.* 13:12ff., esp. v. 16; 17:12; 19:11-13; 21:18-21; 22:21-24; 24:7).

13:6-11 [Heb. 13:7-12]. *Thy brother, the son of thy mother, or thy son, or thy daughter, or the wife of thy bosom, or thy friend* (v. 6). As effective as the wonder-sign of the speaking serpent with its oracular declarations in the case of Eve's seduction was the constraint lent to Eve's subsequent temptation of Adam by his affection for her, flesh of his flesh, wife of his bosom, beloved as his own soul to him. *Entice thee secretly* (v. 6). The subtlety of the temptation in this case contrasts with the public invitation of the false prophet (*cf.* vv. 1ff.) and would make it easy to conceal the dear one's sin and to avoid the judicial responsibility without detection. But, as in the case of the international treaties, any failure to report "evil words" and expose rebellious plots was a breach of the covenant. The call of the covenant is to love the Lord our God though it mean to hate parents and brethren, wife and children, and one's own life also (*cf.* Luke 14:26). Therefore, that one who was dearest to the covenant servant must be as sternly judged as the false prophet if he or she proposed disloyalty to Yahweh. *Neither shall thine eye pity him . . . But thou shalt surely kill him* (vv. 8, 9). For the judicial procedure in view (vv. 9, 10), see 17:7. An important benefit of executing the divine sentence would be the monitory impact on Israel, forestalling further apostasy (v. 11; *cf.* 17:13; 19:20; 21:21).

13:12-18 [Heb. 13:13-19]. *One of thy cities* (v. 12). If the stipulations of the preceding verses were not vigorously carried out, the rebellion would increase from individual to community proportions, a situation requiring the yet more difficult judicial decision and action prescribed here. In verse 13, *base fellows* (ASV and RSV) and *children of Belial* (AV) are renderings of an expression variously understood as sons of worthlessness or disorder or wickedness or Sheol. This is how God sees those enticers to idolatry who appeared to men as impressive prophets or dearest kin. *Smite . . . destroying it utterly* (v. 15). If the verdict of guilt was reached (v. 14), the sentence must be the infliction of the ban (*cf.* comments on 7:1-5). By embracing the abomination of Canaan, the Israelite city would become an abomination; it would become like Canaanite Jericho and must share Jericho's cursed doom by fire and sword (v. 15). *You shall gather all its spoil into the midst of its open square, and burn the city and all its spoil with fire, as a whole burnt offering to the Lord your God* (v. 16, RSV). As did the human lords in their ancient treaties, Israel's divine Suzerain imposed regulations concerning the spoil that would fall into the hands of his vassal on a punitive campaign. In the present instance, the less common demand was made that all the spoil be added to the holocaust by which the accursed city became a whole burnt offering to the praise of God's justice and wrath. *A heap forever* (v. 16); the Hebrew *tēl* denotes the abandoned mound produced by the accumulating debris of successive occupations of a site. Israel's experience in the case of Achan (Josh. 7 and 8) exemplified both the danger of violating the law of the spoil in verses 16, 17a and the faithfulness of the Lord to the promise of verses 17b, 18.

c. FILIAL OBLIGATIONS, 14:1-15:23

Chapter 14. As the people of Yahweh, committed to his service and commissioned to remove from their midst all devotees and shrines of idols (Deut. 12 and 13), Israel was a distinctive nation. That must be manifested throughout the ceremonial dimension of the nation's life. Whether in connection with death (vv. 1, 2) or life (vv. 3-21), the ceremonial practice of the people must reflect their peculiar sanctity. Their sacred consecration was also to be displayed in the consecration of the fruit of their life's labor to the Lord their God (vv. 22-29).

14:1, 2. *Ye are the children of the Lord your God* (v. 1). Here again the Exodus 19:5, 6 definition of the theocratic nation is echoed (*cf.* 7:6), enriched now with the concept of sonship (*cf.* Ex. 4:22). In the Old Testament period the emphasis was on Israel as servant rather than as son, because though Israel was the son and heir, it was under governors until the time appointed of the Father (*cf.* Gal. 4:1ff.). The Israelites were not to mutilate themselves as the heathen commonly did in mourning rites (v. 1b; *cf.* Lev. 19:28; 21:5). The reason assigned (v. 2) was that theirs was a holy status as the elect and adopted people of God, and underlying that reason was the fact that their God was the Lord of life, who had created man in his image.

14:3-21. *Thou shalt not eat any abominable thing* (v. 3). Ceremonial distinctions may at times appear arbitrary. Such is the case with the classification of clean and unclean meats in these dietary regulations, for hygienic explanations are apparent only in some, not in all instances. But the very arbitrariness of these stipulations made them the better tests of submission to the sovereign word of the Lord and more distinctive badges of consecration to him. It reminded Israel that man must live according to every word of God's mouth (*cf.* 8:3). It is God's creative word that gives to all things their definition and meaning, and man must interpret all things according to the interpretation God assigns them. In this respect the Mosaic dietary rules resembled the probationary proscription of the fruit of the tree of knowledge in Eden, or the arrangements for the provision of the manna in the wilderness.

These are the animals you may eat (v. 4, RSV). This section repeats almost verbally Leviticus 11:2-23. Deuteronomy 14:4b, 5 supplements the Levitical formulation and that in a way which reflects the wilderness origin of Deuteronomy. For the habitat of the edible game animals specified was the area of Israel's journeying from Egypt to Canaan, not the wooded hill country of Canaan itself. Verse 21a involves a modification of Leviticus 17:15. The practice of boiling a kid in its mother's milk (v. 21b; *cf.* Ex. 23:19; 34:26) was prohibited because it was a ceremonial custom of the Canaanites.

14:22-29. *Thou shalt truly tithe all the increase of thy seed* (v. 22). An annual tithe of the produce of the land was to be offered to Yahweh in recognition that the land was his and that he was the Bestower of life and fertility. Because of variants between the Deuteronomic and the earlier tithe stipulations (see Lev. 27:30-33; Num. 18:21-32), the erroneous view was developed by the Jews (and has been accepted by many Christian exegetes) that Deuteronomy prescribes a second tithe and, some would say, even a third tithe (*cf.* Deut. 14:28ff.; 26:12-15). Deuteronomy 14 does not, however, necessarily involve any drastic modification of the earlier tithe law. It specifies only an agricultural tithe, though it mentions the firstlings of flock and herd (v. 23; *cf.* 12:17; 15:19ff.). But even Numbers 18 does not explicitly mention an animal tithe. Only Leviticus 27 does so (*cf.* II Chr. 31:6). It is possibly taken for granted in

both Numbers 18 and Deuteronomy 14. According to Numbers
18:21, "every tithe" (RSV) was given to the Levites. Deuteronomy 14 specifies that except in the third and sixth years
(and of course the fallow sabbath year also, cf. Ex. 23:11) the
offerer might use the tithe, presumably, however, only a small
part of it, for a communion feast at the sanctuary. A minor
modification (in keeping with the familiar charitable interest
of the Mosaic legislation in the poor class which would emerge
in the social stratification of life in Canaan) was the inclusion
of other dependents along with the Levites in the use of the
tithe of the third and sixth years (v. 29). *That thou mayest
learn to fear the Lord thy God always* (v. 23). The purpose of
this section is not so much to give a comprehensive statement
of the tithe law as to guard tithing procedure from being pros-
tituted to idolatrous ends; that is, to prevent Israel from
honoring the Canaanite fertility deities for their harvests. The
insistence, therefore, is that all religious ceremony associated
with tithing be conducted at Yahweh's central sanctuary (v.
23; cf. 12:6, 11). It is necessary to take account of this particular
purpose of these verses when making comparisons with tithing
regulations elsewhere. On the reason for the permission of
verses 24ff., cf. 12:21. *At the end of three years* (v. 28); the
conjunction of this with the sabbatical legislation of 15:1ff.
indicates that such triennial years (called in 26:12 "the year
of tithing") were the third and sixth years within the sabbatical-
Jubilee cycle. See Numbers 18:26-32 for the disposition of
these tithes to be made by the Levites.

Chapter 15. The main thread of the preceding legislation is
picked up again in the law of the firstlings in 15:19-23 (cf.
14:23). Meanwhile, verses 1-18 elaborate the subject of love
toward needy brethren which came up in the exposition of tithing
procedure (14:27ff.). Specifically, these stipulations deal with
the remission of debts (vv. 1-11) and the manumission of bond
servants (vv. 12-18). A further element of continuity is found in
the sabbatical framework for this program of mercy (cf. 14:28).

15:1-11. *At the end of every seven years* (v. 1). This refers
to the sabbatical year which ended each seven-year period
within a Jubilee cycle (cf. 14:28). The institution of the year
of release was established in the Book of the Covenant (Ex.
23:10, 11) and expounded in the Levitical instructions (Lev.
25:2ff.). *The Lord's release* (v.2); the Hebrew *sh⁽ᵉ⁾miṭṭâ*,
"release," comes from a root meaning "to let fall." In Exodus

23:11 it is applied to the land in the sense of lying fallow; hence the year of release is "a sabbath of rest unto the land" (Lev. 25:4). Here it is applied to debts in the sense of remission. Many have interpreted this as a one-year moratorium on the creditor's collection of debts. However, the fact that the seventh year of release and the Jubilee year of liberty belonged to one symbolical unit indicates that a permanent cancelation of debts is meant. The crowning Jubilee Sabbath simply carried the principle further to a restoration of personal freedom and a reversion of real estate to its original owners. At each level the sabbatical release is a renewal of Yahweh's original deliverance of the covenant people from bondage and a reinstatement of the families in their original inheritance. Agreeably, the Sabbath itself is associated with the Lord's deliverance of his needy, crying people from bondage (*cf.* Deut. 5:14, 15). The release of the seventh year was the Lord's though his mercy was manifested through the philanthropy of his servants. It was designed to refurbish the theocratic symbol of the kingdom of God periodically by a fresh realization of the saving and restoring grace of God which was experienced so abundantly at the beginning of Israel's theocratic life. It is interesting to observe that certain Babylonian kings proclaimed general releases in the first year of their reign. The Old Testament's seventh year release also pointed prophetically to the future redemptive action of God, anticipating the messianic reign of mercy to the poor and helpless (*cf.* Ps. 72). This consummation prospect is always present in sabbatical symbolism. *But there will be no poor among you* (v. 4, RSV). It is parenthetically observed (vv. 4-6) that the need for charity would be obviated by the absence of any poor in Israel, if the faithfulness were always manifested which would warrant the bestowal of the covenant's blessings in richest measure. As a matter of fact, however, for want of fidelity in Israel, the poor would be always present (v. 11; *cf.* Mark 14:7). *Take heed lest . . . your eye be hostile to your poor brother* (v. 9, RSV). Such indeed were the sinful propensities of even the chosen people that they must be warned lest this septennial provision of mercy to the poor become an occasion for oppressing them in the intervening periods. The practice of a year of release seems to some financially infeasible (which is one reason why some commentators interpret the release as a temporary suspension of debt). But the people of faith were called upon to recognize that within the peculiar covenantal arrangements of God with the theocratic nation, obedience to this stipulation was a guarantee of prosperity: *For this thing the Lord thy God shall bless thee in all thy works* (v. 10; cf. Lev. 25:20, 21). That the Scriptures do not recommend this as a normative policy outside the Old Testament theocratic community of Israel is evident even from the exceptive clause in verse 3a. The *foreigner* (v. 3a) is not, like the "sojourner" or "stranger who is within thy gates," a permanent member of the community, but one temporarily visiting for commercial purposes or the like.

15:12-18. *In the seventh year thou shalt let him go free* (v. 12). Though septennially structured, this law of the Hebrew servant, unlike the legislation in 14:28, 29 and 15:1-11, does not refer to the regular sabbatical units within a Jubilee cycle. The seven-year period it deals with began whenever an individual Hebrew became an indentured servant. This provision for manumission was also contained in the Book of the Covenant (Ex. 21:2-6) and finds a counterpart within the Levitical legislation concerning the Jubilee year (Lev. 25:39-55; cf. Jer. 34:14). *Or an Hebrew woman* (v. 12). The inclusion of Hebrew women, possibly implicit in Exodus 21:2-6 (cf. Ex. 21:7-11, which is concerned with the special case of the concubine-maidservant) becomes explicit here. As in the release of debt, so in the release of the slave, the limits of application were the Israelite brotherhood.

In view of the contrast instituted between the "brother" and "foreigner" in this context and the identification of the Hebrew servant as a brother (v. 12), the theory which regards the "Hebrew servant" as a "foreign servant" must be judged erroneous. According to that theory, what Exodus 21:6 and Deuteronomy 15:17 allow for a Hebrew servant, Leviticus 25:44-46 forbids for an Israelite. But Leviticus 25 refers to a compulsory, rigorous slavery, while the Hebrew servant passages refer to a voluntary, agreeable service. The stipulation of a Jubilee manumission in Leviticus 25:40, 41 supplements the Hebrew servant's right of seventh-year release as a special boon when the Jubilee arrived before his seventh year of service. This supplementary right, like that of release in the seventh year, was subject to the servant's further right to voluntary lifelong service of a beloved master (Ex. 21:5, 6; Deut. 15:16, 17).

Thou shalt furnish him liberally (v. 14). In this Deuteronomic reformulation of the provision it becomes more generous (vv.

13, 14), and various inducements to obedience are cited (vv. 15, 18).

15:19-23. The subject of firstlings mentioned in 14:23 (*cf.* 12:6, 17) is here resumed. Earlier legislation on the subject is found in Exodus 13:2, 11-16; 22:29, 30; 34:19, 20; Leviticus 27:26, 27; Numbers 18:15-18. The Deuteronomic treatment is not exhaustive but designed only to clarify the relevance of the law of the central altar (Deut. 12) to the administration of the law of firstlings within the anticipated circumstances of the tribes dispersed and exposed to the dangerous influences of local Canaanite shrines. *Thou shalt eat it before the Lord thy God year by year in the place which the Lord shall choose* (v. 20). This new formulation refers to a fact not noted in previous legislation, namely, that the offerer and his household were to participate in the sacrificial meal accompanying the presentation of firstlings. Clearly, that is mentioned here in order to press the requirement that all sacred feasting must take place at the central sanctuary (*cf.* 12:6, 17), even though in Canaan common feasts would be permitted elsewhere (*cf.* 12:15ff.). There is no necessary contradiction between the assignment of the first-lings to the priests and their families (Num. 18:15-18) and this sharing of the offerer's family in the sacrificial meal. See 14:23-27 for a similar situation with respect to the disposition of the tithes. Annual offering was substituted for eight-day offering (*cf.* Ex. 22:30) for the same reason that eating of flesh at home was henceforth to be allowed (*cf.* 12:21). On verse 21a, *cf.* Leviticus 22:19ff.; Deuteronomy 17:1. Observe again in verses 22, 23 the concern to show the relevance of the funda-mental legislation of Deuteronomy 12 to this particular matter of the firstlings (*cf.* 12:15f., 22ff.).

d. TRIBUTARY PILGRIMAGES, 16:1-17

The section which began at 12:1 concludes with command-ments concerning the three annual pilgrimages to the central sanctuary: the feasts of Passover and Unleavened Bread (vv. 1-8), Weeks (vv. 9-12), and Tabernacles (vv. 13-15). For the earlier legislation, see chiefly Exodus 12; Leviticus 23; Numbers 28 and 29. Our comments here are largely devoted to features peculiar to the Deuteronomic formulation and problems raised thereby. The sabbatical scheme is again present (*cf.* 14:28-15:18) for the entire religious calendar of feasts was sabbatically patterned. Still prominent is the concern with the way in which the contemplated divine choice of a permanent sanctuary site in the midst of an extensive land must modify previous ceremonial practice. Note the repeated use of the formula for the central altar (vv. 2, 6, 7, 11, 15, 16). Because Deuteronomy is a covenant renewal document presupposing earlier covenant stipulations as still valid, except as it expressly modifies them, it condenses and omits much while giving new emphasis to features affected by the introduction of "the place which the Lord will choose." Recognition of this should have prevented many of the higher critical allegations of contradiction between Deuteronomy and other Pentateuchal legislation. Viewed as part of a suzerainty treaty, Deuteronomy 16:1-17 corresponds to the customary demand that the vassal appear annually before the suzerain with the stipulated tribute. Beginning with verse 18 there is a new section principally concerned with the administration of justice.

16:1-8. The Passover. *Observe the month of Abib* (v. 1). On the date, *cf.* Exodus 12:1, 6; 34:18. *The passover* (vv. 1, 2). As used in these verses, the term "passover" comprehends both the Passover proper and the following seven-day feast of Unleavened Bread. See verse 3, noting that the antecedent of *therewith* is *passover* (v. 2). Consequently, this Passover sacrifice might be taken from both flock and herd (v. 2), whereas for the Passover proper a lamb was prescribed (Ex. 12:3ff.). For the sacrifices referred to in verse 2, see the account of the celebration in II Chronicles 30:22ff. and 35:7ff., and note the use there of the term "passover offerings," lit. "passovers," for sacrifices from the herd. In order to designate more specifically the Passover proper, Moses called it *the flesh which you sacrifice on the evening of the first day* (v. 4). The references to the "passover" immediately after that designation (vv. 5, 6) are also evidently to be taken in that narrower sense. *Thou shalt roast and eat it* (v. 7). The RSV unnecessarily creates a conflict with Exodus 12:9 by translating the verb *bāshal* as "boil," rather than "roast," as in AV and ASV. It is only an additional specification, like "with water" or "in pots," that definitely gives this verb the meaning "boil" (*cf.* Ex. 12:9; II Chr. 35:13b). When further defined by "with fire," *bāshal* clearly signifies "roast" (*cf.* II Chr. 35:13a). By itself it is ambiguous. This ambiguity is allowed in Deuteronomy 16:7 because the manner of preparing the sacrifice for eating had already been established and is not Moses' present concern. He is here laboring the point that this feast must take place at the central sanctuary (vv. 2, 6, 7). Only after the complete observance of the feast, both preparation and participation, might the worshipers depart from the sanctuary to their living quarters (v. 7b). *Unto thy tents* (v. 7). The ambiguity of this expression (which would here refer to the pilgrims' temporary quarters in the holy city) is also attributable to Moses' overriding interest in the idea of the central altar. Preparation of the sacrifice at the sanctuary was a modification of the observance of the first Passover in Egypt; there the blood was applied to the individual homes in the absence of a centralized cult and altar. The *bread of affliction* (v. 3) recalled the oppressive circumstances in the house of bondage, especially pharaoh's opposition to Israel's departure, which compelled their hasty preparations for flight. On verses 3, 4a, *cf.* Exodus 12:15, 18-20; 13:3, 6, 7; 23:15; 34:18; Leviticus 23:6. On verse 4b, *cf.* Exodus 12:10; 23:18b; 34:25b; Numbers 9:12. On verse 8, *cf.* Exodus 12:16; Leviticus 23:7, 8; Numbers 28:18, 25.

16:9-12. The Feast of Weeks. On the subject of this section, see the earlier prescriptions in Exodus 23:16; 34:22; Leviticus 23:15ff.; Numbers 28:26ff. The *feast of weeks* (v. 10; *cf.* Ex. 34:22) was also called "feast of harvest" (Ex. 23:16) and "day of the firstfruits" (Num. 28:26). In later times it received the Greek name Pentecost because of the way its date was calculated, namely, fifty days from a set starting point (*cf.* Lev. 23:16). That point is here described in general terms as the beginning of the grain harvest (v. 9). There was no need for greater precision because the exact date had already been given in Leviticus 23:10ff. It was the second day of the feast of Unleavened Bread, the day of the offering of the sheaf of the firstfruits of the grain harvest. This was the "morrow after the sabbath" (Lev. 23:15), for the first day of Unleavened Bread was a day of rest (Lev. 23:7; *cf.* Josh. 5:11). Following this reckoning, the New Testament Pentecost event would fall on a Saturday. The seven weeks between the Passover and Harvest pilgrimages allowed time for the completion of the grain harvest. *Free-will offering* (v. 10); *cf.* Numbers 29:39; Leviticus 23:38. This feast was one of joy — joy in the Lord who had brought his people unto their fruitful paradise land (vv. 10b, 11; *cf.* 12:7, 12, 18; 16:14, 15) — joy in the Lord who had delivered from bondage (v. 12), and thus a joy to be shared with all the poor within the covenant family (v. 11b). And this joyous festival was to be held at the central sanctuary (v. 11).

16:13-15. The Feast of Tabernacles. Parallel legislation is in Exodus 23:16; 34:22; Leviticus 23:33ff., Numbers 29:12ff. The *feast of tabernacles* (v. 13), or *booths* (RSV), is also called the "feast of ingathering" (in the Exodus legislation). Like the feast of Unleavened Bread, it lasted a week, *i.e.*, from the fifteenth to the twenty-first of the seventh month. It was followed by an octave sabbath day (*cf.* Lev. 23:36, 39). The name Tabernacles reflects the custom of dwelling in booths during the festival, which served as a memorial of life in the wilderness (*cf.* the use of unleavened bread). The name Ingathering indicates that this feast was the culmination of the agricultural year, when vintage as well as grain had been harvested. In the year of release, when there was no harvest, this feast was the occasion for the significant public reading of the text of the covenant (31:9-13). Once again, the point of the Deuteronomic formulation is to enforce the law of the central sanctuary (v. 15). Here, too, joy and love are the marks of covenant life and worship (v. 14).

16:16, 17. *Cf.* Exodus 23:17; 34:23. This concluding summary, turning all eyes again to the central sanctuary (v. 16a), brings into relief the character of the pilgrimages as tributary trips to the throne of the God-King (v. 16b). *According to the blessing of the Lord* (v. 17); *cf.* I Corinthians 16:2.

2. JUDICIAL-GOVERNMENTAL RIGHTEOUSNESS, 16:18-21:23

This section contains a series of stipulations concerning theocratic government, with primary emphasis on the judiciary. Israel must add to cultic holiness political-judicial righteousness. Between the governmental and the cultic there was a unity of ultimate authority since Yahweh was both God and King in Israel. Consequently, all theocratic institutions, unlike those in the ordinary state, were confessionally religious and there was an extension of cultic praxis beyond the sanctuary into governmental administration. Moreover, because all theocratic law, moral and civil as well as cultic, was comprehended in the covenant stipulations of Yahweh which were inscripturated in the covenant document, and because that Book of the Law was committed to the priests at the central sanctuary to be guarded and expounded by them, the priesthood possessed the dominant judicial voice (*cf.* 21:5), at least until the beginning of the monarchy (*cf.* 17:9, 10). In addition to their knowledge of the written law, the priests had access by Urim and Thummim to direct divine verdicts. That would afford to the priests a more ultimate role even though kings became more prominent in the judicial process. Abroad in the land the oracular voice of the divine King enthroned in the sanctuary was increasingly revealed to and through the prophet. But while prophets registered the Lord's unsought judgments upon the vassal people and leadership, the judicial functioning of the priest was related to litigation instituted by one Israelite vassal against another or to legal investigations initiated within the Israelite community.

a. Judges and God's Altar, 16:18-17:13

The law of the Lord must be administered with justice (16:18-20); therefore, judicial procedures calculated to promote the interests of truth must be practiced (17:2-7). In this sphere of the court, the Lord God of Israel must be recognized as the exclusive source of authority (16:21-17:1), and agreeably the officers who represented him at his central sanctuary constituted the highest theocratic judicatory (17:8-13).

16:18-20. During the wilderness journeying Moses the mediator had been Israel's judge, with assistant judges from the tribes appointed to handle the ordinary cases (*cf.* 1:12ff.; Ex. 18:13ff.). That arrangement is here modified to meet the new conditions of life in Canaan. *In all thy gates* (v. 18). The judicial districts there were to be the towns rather than tribal-genealogical divisions. The natural leaders of the local council of elders would probably be the judges and assistant officers who are in view here (*cf.* 19:12). *Justice, justice shalt thou follow* (v. 20, Hebrew literally). In this introduction to the subject the emphasis falls, however, not on the organizational structure of the judicatories but on the demand for justice in administering the law of Yahweh (vv. 19, 20; *cf.* Ex. 23:3, 6, 8). Even in the codes and epics of Israel's heathen neighbors the virtue of justice in leaders is an often reiterated ideal.

16:21-17:1. The interlocking of cultic and governmental processes (see the introductory comments on 16:18-21:23 above) explains the appearance of cultic proscriptions among the judicial regulations. These verses propound in concrete fashion the regulative religious principles found in the first three laws of the Decalogue; these were to characterize judicial procedure. First, the authority of Yahweh alone must be consulted (vv. 21, 22; *cf.* 17:8-10). This is expressed negatively in the prohibition of idolatrous appeal for oracular decision (*cf.* 18:9-14).

Asherah (v. 21, RSV; "grove," AV), the Canaanite goddess, had as one significant epithet, "Asherah of deposits, goddess of oracles" (*Keret*, 201, 202). Apparently then, the cultic Asherah and pillar were symbols associated with judicial procedure, specifically, with the delivering of oracular verdict (*cf*. Prov. 16:10). Such a role was played by images of gods in Egypt, especially in the New Kingdom. Second, the cultic aspect of judicial procedure must be characterized by the same reverence for Yahweh's holy name that was required in all Israel's cultic service (17:1; *cf*. 15:21; 21:1ff.; Lev. 22:17ff.).

17:2-7. Beginning here, rules of evidence and judgment are presented. The particular case of apostasy which is cited (vv. 2, 3) is simply illustrative of cases requiring capital punishment as the verdict. Concrete rather than abstract formulation of principles is a feature of the Deuteronomic legislation. For the stipulations concerned with apostasy as such, see Deuteronomy 13 (*cf*. Ex. 22:20). The selection of this particular illustration is appropriate for it underscores the contextual emphasis on the exclusive lordship of Yahweh in the judicial process. *In transgressing his covenant* (v. 2); the prohibition of foreign allegiance (*cf*. v. 3) is the recurring, basic prohibition of the covenant. *Which I have not commanded* (v. 3); the first person form reminds us that Moses spoke as the mouth of Yahweh (*cf*. 1:3; 7:4). *Then shalt thou inquire diligently* (v. 4, ASV). The central point is the demand that justice be safeguarded by a conscientiously thorough investigation (*cf*. 13:14) and insistence on adequate evidence (vv. 6, 7; *cf*. 19:15). A minimum of two witnesses was required (*cf*. Num. 35:30) and their confidence in their own testimony was to be evidenced by their assuming the dread responsibility of delivering the first and quite possibly lethal blows in the execution of the condemned (*cf*. 13:9). This measure also prevented secret accusation in prosecution of private quarrels. *Bring forth . . . unto thy gates* (v. 5). The execution occurred outside the camp (*cf*. Lev. 24:14; Num. 15:36; Heb. 13:12).

17:8-13. Moses perpetuated in modified form the system of lower and higher judicatories which had been instituted at Sinai (*cf*. Ex. 18:13ff.). During the wanderings both Moses, the final arbiter, and the body of judges assisting in less weighty matters held court in the vicinity of the sanctuary. Since, however, the lower courts would henceforth be decentralized and located throughout the towns of Israel (*cf*. 16:18), it is here specified that the higher tribunal was to continue at the sanctuary at *the place which the Lord thy God shall choose* (v. 8), a reminder that he who dwelt at the sanctuary was Israel's supreme Judge. This arrangement was designed in the first instance for the pre-monarchial period but it could be continued after the rise of a king in Israel (*cf.* vv. 14ff.; II Chr. 19:8ff.). *Thou shalt come unto the priests the Levites, and unto the judge that shall be in those days, and enquire; and they shall show thee the sentence of judgment* (v. 9). Any variety of case which proved *too hard* (v. 8a, literally "too wonderful," *cf.* Job 42:3) for the local court came under the jurisdiction of the court at the central sanctuary (*cf.* 19:16-18). The latter was not a court of appeal, however. The central judicature consisted of a plurality of both priests and judges (*cf.* 19:17), but each of these groups had its individual head, *viz*, the high priest (*cf.* v. 12) and a "chief justice." The formulation is not specific enough to determine from this ordinance the exact division of responsibility between priest and judge (*cf.* II Chr. 19:11). Apparently, verdicts might be announced by either priest or judge. Since the decision was in either case delivered by the representative of Yahweh it must be scrupulously followed (vv. 10, 11). *The man that . . . will not hearken . . . shall die* (v. 12). Any failure to comply was rebellion against Yahweh himself and was liable to the death penalty. Indeed, these representatives of Yahweh, as the official agents of his judgment, are denominated *'ĕlōhîm*, "gods," (AV, "judges") in Exodus 21:6; 22:8, 28 (in the latter, note the parallelism with "ruler of thy people"). On verse 13, *cf.* 13:11.

b. KINGS AND GOD'S COVENANT, 17:14-20

Like the law of the stationary sanctuary, this law of the king envisages not the immediate but more distant future (17:14). Though the establishment of a monarchy is presented not as mandatory but as permissible, that is sufficient to show that a monarchy as such need not be antithetical to the principle of theocratic government (*cf.* Gen. 17:6, 16; 35:11; 49:10). All depended on the kind of monarchy that should emerge. If the king conformed to the spirit of the present provision, ruling under Yahweh and by the covenant law, he would actually enrich the Old Testament's symbolic prefiguration of the messianic reign. It was the indifference of Israel to the religious requisites for a theocratic king that accounted for Samuel's opposition to their request for a king (*cf.* I Sam. 8:4ff.). It is noteworthy that in the secular suzerainty treaties a similar oversight of the vassal's choice of king is exercised.

17:14-20. The main insistence of this passage, which lays the legal-covenantal foundation for the later monarchy, is that even when dynastic kingship will have replaced charismatic judgeship the kings, too, must subject their life and reign, particularly their judicial activity, to Yahweh's covenant (vv. 18-20). The judicial supremacy belonged to the Lord, whose law was under the guardianship of the priests (v. 18; *cf.* v. 11).

Whom the Lord thy God shall choose (v. 15). The divine choice of a king to sit on the throne of Yahweh (*cf.* I Chr. 29:23) was revealed through a prophet (*cf.* I Sam. 10:24; 16: 12ff.). *One from among thy brethren* (v. 15). He was to be a fellow covenant servant. In this respect the king would be like his messianic antitype. The restrictions of verses 16, 17 reflect conditions in the royal courts of the nations around Israel. In some of these the king was a god; in Israel, God was King (*cf.* Ex. 15:18; 19:5,6; Deut. 33:5; Judg. 8:23). On verse 16b, *cf.* Exodus 13:17; 14:13; Deuteronomy 28:68. In the wilderness the Israelites longed for the agricultural produce of Egypt (*cf.* Num. 11:5, 18, 20; 14:4); confronted by empires in which horses were a source of economic and military strength, they would lust for the pharaoh's famed horses and chariots (*cf.* Isa. 30:2; I Kgs. 10:28, 29), forgetting the import of their election and deliverance from Egyptian bondage. For the Solomonic violation of these restrictions, *cf.* I Kings 10:26ff.; 11:1ff. *And it shall be, when he sitteth upon the throne of his kingdom, that he shall write him a copy of this law in a book* (v. 18). A duplicate copy of suzerainty treaties was provided for each vassal king. The Lord's copy, here regarded as the original and standard, was deposited at the central sanctuary (*cf.* 31:9). On verses 19, 20, *cf.* 31:12, 13. David manifested the conformity of his spirit to this covenantal law of kingship by his psalmodic response to it (see, *e.g.*, Ps. 1 and 19) and by locating his throne site near the central sanctuary at the place which God had chosen.

c. Priests and Prophets, 18:1-22

Responsibility is laid upon Israel for the support of the priestly ministers of God whose administrative assignments are cited in the preceding and following contexts (vv. 1-8). Then

Moses enjoins the elimination of all false oracular claimants, including the false prophet (vv. 9-22). In that connection, the institution of the true prophets is set forth (vv. 15ff.), rounding out the treatment of theocratic leaders (*cf.* judge, 16:8; king, 17:14ff.; priest and Levite, 18:1ff.) which is appropriately incorporated into this section of legislation dealing with the official administration of righteousness in theocratic life.

18:1-8. *The priests the Levites* (v. 1). Deuteronomy uses this designation five times and "priests the sons of Levi" twice, and seven times it uses simply "priest(s)." *And all the tribe of Levi* (v. 1). The *and* is interpretive since in Hebrew the construction is one of simple juxtaposition. This interpretation is grammatically acceptable (see Deut. 17:1; *cf.* 15:21) and consistent with the representation in the rest of the Scriptures, according to which all the priests were descended from Levi but only Aaronite Levites were priests. The RSV translation, "that is, all the tribe of Levi," foists on Deuteronomy the view that all Levites were priests and thereby creates a conflict between it and the other biblical legislation. Deuteronomy itself conveys a distinctly different image of each group. The priests are the altar ministers of the central sanctuary; they enjoy a position of supreme honor and authority. The Levites are everywhere functional subordinates and social dependents. Priests and Levites did share the commission of instructing Israel in the covenant law (*cf.* 33:10a; Lev. 10:11; II Chr. 15:3; 17:8, 9; 30:22; 35:3).

No part nor inheritance (v. 1). That is, they would possess no unified tribal territory (*cf.* 10:9; 12:12; 14:27, 29). As compact formulations serving the purposes of treaty renewal, the Deuteronomic stipulations assume the validity of the more minute regulations given earlier, unless of course they expressly modify them. So here, verses 1b, 2 allude to legislation like Numbers 18:20ff.; Leviticus 2:3; 7:6-10, 28ff. *The Lord is their inheritance* (v. 2). The Lord chose the Levites as his first-born consecration portion of Israel (v. 5; *cf.* Num. 3:5-13) and then gave himself to them as their portion. The latter was expressed in their participation in Israel's offerings to him. The arrangement was symbolic of the great covenantal truth that Yahweh was Israel's God and Israel was Yahweh's people.

This shall be the priests' due from the people (v. 3, ASV). It is a question whether verse 3 further defines the fire-offerings and *inheritance* (*e.g.*, firstfruits, tithes) of verses 1, 2, or appoints certain additional portions. In the former case, there is a modification of earlier law, for the specific parts here assigned to the priests (v. 3b) are not those detailed in Leviticus 7:29ff. If this is correct, an explanation of the modification of the earlier right shoulder requirement might well be that that was the portion given to Canaanite priests, as has been disclosed by the discovery of a pit filled with right shoulder bones in connection with a Canaanite temple. Assuming verse 3 to be supplementary to earlier legislation, some have held that the reference is not to sacrifice but to animals slaughtered at home (*cf.* the terminology in 12:15, 21). Such a provision would prevent the serious diminution of the priests' revenue which would otherwise be the effect of removing this considerable portion of butchery from the category of sacrifice. Another more tenable explanation of verse 3 interpreted as a supplementary provision is that it refers not to the peace offerings proper but to certain other sacred meals eaten at the sanctuary, whether generally festive or, as the present context might suggest, associated with judicial procedure. In verse 4, the fleece supplements earlier requirements (*cf.* Num. 18:12).

If a Levite come from any of thy gates out of all Israel (v. 6). The priests' cities were near Jerusalem, but those of the Levites farther afield (see Josh. 21). Verses 6-8 guarantee the rights of all Levites against any restrictive tendencies of vested priestly interests at the central sanctuary. The charity towards the Levites required of Israel in general was required of the priests too. On the terminology used to describe the Levitical service in verse 7, *cf.* II Chronicles 29:4, 5, 11, 12; 23:6; Deuteronomy 10:8.

18:9-22. If Israel desired further revelation of the will of the Lord in addition to that inscripturated in the law of Moses, the means of Urim and Thummim was available to their priests. Beyond that, the initiative in revelation lay with God who would raise up and speak through prophets (v. 18). Israel must be satisfied with and submissive to Yahweh's revelation (vv. 15-19); if they deemed Moses and the prophets inadequate, then a voice from the dead would not help. Allegedly oracular sources such as flourished among the Canaanites must be shunned (vv. 9-14), and a presumptuous prophet speaking as from Yahweh, indeed, every false prophet, must be exterminated (vv. 20-22).

Thou shalt not learn to do after the abominations of those nations (v. 9). All occult superstitions — divination, sorcery, spiritualism (vv. 10, 11) — were *abominations* (vv. 9, 12) to Yahweh and invited the sentence of the ban (*cf.* comments on 7:1ff.). Pagan magic was identified with pagan religion and therefore its practice would be rebellion against the demand of Yahweh's covenant for Israel's loyalty (*cf.* v. 13, *thou shalt be perfect*).

The Lord thy God will raise up unto thee a prophet from the midst of thee, of thy brethren, like unto me (v. 15). This figure of the prophet, like certain others in the Old Testament (*viz.* the seed of the woman, the son of David, the servant of the Lord, the son of man) has both a corporate and individual significance. The collective sense (*i.e.*, the whole institution of Old Testament prophecy) is clearly required; for the problem of distinguishing true and false prophets is broached in this connection (vv. 20-22), and this "prophet" is presented as the legitimate counterpart to the oracular institutions of Canaan (vv. 9-14). Also, within the structure of Deuteronomy this passage belongs to the section that deals with the several theocratic offices; moreover, the prophetic office is not elsewhere formally instituted. See, too, Luke 11:50, 51. At the same time, this passage was interpreted by Jesus and the apostles as pointing to the Messiah (see especially Acts 3:22, 23; *cf.* John 5:43; 12:48, 49; Matt. 17:5). Jesus was the antitypical prophet whom the Old Testament prophetic institution foreshadowed. The prophetic office was a mediatorial function and so, in measure, an extension of the mediatorial office of Moses (*cf. like unto me*, v. 15; *cf.* Num. 12:6, 7). It was given to Israel in response to the request made at Horeb for a mediator of divine revelation (vv. 16ff.; *cf.* 5:23ff.).

The prophet which shall presume to speak a word in my name (v. 20). This kind of prophet was a more subtle menace than the Canaanite soothsayer or the Israelite, sign-attested dreamer of dreams who enticed to other gods (v. 20b; 13:1ff.), and he was to receive the same treatment as they (v. 20c; *cf.* v. 12; 13:5). Identifying him was more difficult (v. 21), but he would be exposed by the failure of his verifiable predictions (v. 22).

d. GUARANTEES OF JUSTICE, 19:1-21

The theme of judicial justice is continued with stipulations calculated to secure a fair trial and true verdict. Asylum was provided for the manslayer lest the wrath of the avenger prevent sober adjudication (vv. 1-13). Tampering with evidence was prohibited (v. 14). Adequate and honest testimony was required (vv. 15-21). These measures served justice by protecting the innocent, but justice was also to be satisfied by the pitiless punishment of the guilty (vv. 11-13, 19-21).

19:1-13. *Thou shalt separate three cities . . . that every man slayer may flee thither* (vv. 2, 3). The land west of Jordan is in view for, as stated at the conclusion to the historical prologue (4:41-43), Moses had already appointed the three cities for this purpose east of Jordan. Joshua's role in completing the appointment of these cities is a mark of the functional and dynastic oneness of Joshua with Moses (*cf.* Josh. 20). *Lest the avenger of blood pursue . . . and slay him* (v. 6; *cf.* Gen. 4:10ff.). The institution of the avenging of blood by the kinsman redeemer was not necessarily indicative of an ethically primitive society but only of a less complex and less centralized form of government. Ideally, the avenger was to act out of passion for justice. However, because of the possibility of his acting out of mere passion, his office, while continued, was wisely controlled in the new, more highly centralized government established by Deuteronomy. The control was achieved by exploiting and expanding the institution of asylum early associated with the altar (*cf.* Gen. 4:15; Ex. 21:14b).

The essence of this provision was contained in the Sinaitic Book of the Covenant (Ex. 21:12-14) and it was fully expounded in Numbers 35:9-34. Certain refinements are added here in Deuteronomy 19 (*cf.* vv. 3a, 8, 9, and 12), particularly with reference to Israel's future growth in Canaan. In Numbers, these cities which afforded protection to the fleeing manslayer not guilty of premeditated murder (v. 4f.) are called "cities of refuge." Just as the geographical separation of the tribes from the central altar in Canaan required a decentralization of animal slaughter (*cf.* Deut. 12:15ff.), so it required a decentralization of asylum. The fact that the cities of refuge were Levitical cities (*cf.* Josh. 20:7ff. and 21:1ff.) indicates, however, that, unlike animal slaying conducted apart from the central altar, the decentralized asylum did not lose its ceremonially sacred character. Note, too, the integration of this provision with the life of the high priest (Num. 35:25). The cities of refuge were then extensions of the altar as a place of asylum. All this contributes further to the emphasis of this section of laws on the judicial importance of the priesthood and the central altar. Since the altar was Yahweh's dwelling place, one can see in these laws of asylum the Deuteronomic equivalent of the extradition stipulations which figure prominently in the international suzerainty treaties.

Then shalt thou add three cities more (v. 9). Moses looked beyond the near future and the selection of the three western cities to a more remote future when Israelite expansion in accordance with the divine promise (cf. 1:7; 11:24; 12:20) would necessitate nine instead of six cities of refuge. There is no historical notice of compliance with this command. *The elders of his city* (v. 12a). These local authorities had the responsibility for innocent blood shed in their vicinity (cf. 21:3ff.) and were therefore given a place in satisfying the cry of that blood for justice (cf. v. 13), but without abrogating the ancient right of the individual avenger (v. 12b). The trial itself was conducted before "the congregation" (cf. Num. 35:12, 24), *i.e.*, before a formal theocratic assembly, and apparently in the locality of the homicide (cf. Num. 35:25; Josh. 20:6). Joshua 20:4 mentions a preliminary hearing which was to be held at the city of refuge upon the fugitive's arrival there.

19:14. This verse deals with what was in effect a violation of the ninth commandment, as do also verses 16-21. *Thy neighbor's landmark* (v. 14a). The value of boundary marks as evidence in property litigation is apparent. Their inviolability was protected by severe sanctions in the various ancient legal codes and by curses against molestors inscribed on the landmarks themselves (cf. 27:17). Stones several feet high (called in Akkadian, *kudurru*) marked the boundaries of royal grants. The fact that the inheritance of Israel and of each individual Israelite was such a royal grant from their divine King would add to the culpability of any who at a future time should tamper with the landmarks that would have been established by the earliest generations after the conquest (*i.e.*, *they of old time*).

19:15-21. *At the mouth of two witnesses, or at the mouth of three witnesses, shall the matter be established* (v. 15). This stipulates as a general principle of administration in criminal cases the law of witness which had earlier been enunciated for capital cases (cf. 17:6, Num. 35:30). Verses 16-21 deal with the perjured witness, that is, with the violation of the ninth commandment in court (cf. 5:20; Ex. 20:16; 23:1). *If a false witness rise up against any man* (v. 16). He is thus designated in view of the outcome, but from the standpoint of the local judges it is not clear whether he or the defendant is the liar. It is precisely because of this difficulty that they refer the case to the central court (*cf*. 17:8-13). *The judges shall make diligent inquisition* (v. 18; *cf*. 13:14; 17:4). There was no resort to ordeal, as in some such cases in the legal practice of Israel's neighbors. *Life for life* (v. 20). The penalty for perjury, however, was to be set according to the principle of the *lex talionis* (*cf*. Ex. 21:23ff.; Lev. 24:17ff.), which was almost universally followed. That principle was not a license to vengeance but a guarantee of justice. Note again the pre-eminence of the priest in judgment (v. 17).

e. JUDGMENT OF THE NATIONS, 20:1-20

Theocratic justice must be exercised in the prosecution of war beyond Israel's borders as well as in the administration of criminal law within the land. Here again a hegemony of priest and cult appears in the judicial process (vv. 2ff.). Just as the cities of refuge were an extension of the asylum aspect of the altar throughout the land (*cf*. 19:1ff.), so the consecrated military campaign against the foreign foe was the just and holy judgment of the sanctuary — or better, of Yahweh — abroad in the earth (vv. 1b, 4, 13a). While all Israelite military operations sanctioned by the Lord were theocratic judgments and the adversary always assumed the character of enemy of God's kingdom, a distinction was made between wars waged against the Canaanite nations and those against nations *very far off* (vv. 15ff.). The programmatic mandate of Deuteronomy 7 concentrated on the former; the present stipulations, on the latter. In the extra-biblical suzerainty treaties, too, the vassal's military activities and share of the spoil were carefully regulated and the suzerain promised support if needed.

20:1-4. *When thou goest out to battle . . . the Lord thy God is with thee* (v. 1). The memory of Yahweh's almighty exploits in establishing the theocracy and the assurance of his presence in their midst even as they waged his holy wars were to provide the fuel for the fire of Israel's faith in the face of superior hosts and military technology. As for horses and chariots, let Israel sing anew the Song of the Sea: "The Lord is a man of war . . . Pharaoh's chariots and his host hath he cast into the sea . . . the horse and the rider hath he thrown into the sea . . . the Lord shall reign for ever and ever" (Ex. 15:3a, 4a, 21b, 18). *The priest shall approach and speak* (v. 2). Priests and interpreters of omens were regular members of military staffs in the ancient world (*cf.* Num. 10:8, 9; 31:6; I Sam. 7:9ff.). The function of the Israelite priest was not analogous to that of a modern army chaplain. He rather represented the sanctuary in the name of which the Israelite host advanced; he consecrated the battle to the glory of the Lord of hosts and of his covenant kingdom. On verse 4, *cf.* 23:14; I Samuel 14:18; II Samuel 11:11.

20:5-9. The situation envisaged here is that of the early days in Canaan before there would be a regular army with foreign mercenaries as an elite corps. The militia of the tribes would be levied by tribal officers (v. 5; *cf.* 1:15). The Assyrian Shamshi-Adad in his military correspondence commands those in charge of the levy: "The chief whose forces are not turned out in full and who leaves one man behind will incur the disfavor of the king" (*Mari*, I, 6:18ff.). Since, however, in the wars of Yahweh, victory came not by the might of Israel's hosts, recruiting was made so free of compulsion that only conscience fortified by faith in Yahweh as the Giver of victory (*cf.* v. 4) compelled enlistment. (For striking historic exemplification of the principle, see Judg. 7:2, 3). *Lest his brethren's heart faint* (v. 8). The Homeric epics depict demoralized troops weeping like calves and wailing like children for home. Such behavior in the Israelite army would disgrace the name of Yahweh before the heathen. The types of exemption cited in verses 5-7 were evidently not novel in Israel. (*Cf.* the Sumerian poem, *Gilgamesh and the Land of the Living*, 49ff.; the Ugaritic poem, *Keret*, 101ff.) Jesus insisted that such excuses as availed for exemption from military service might not prevent a man's responding promptly to his invitation to salvation (see Luke 14:18ff.). On verse 6, *cf.* Leviticus 19:23ff. On verse 7, *cf.* 24:5.

20:10-20. *Proclaim peace unto it* (v. 10b). Such an offer was expressly forbidden in the conflict with the cities of Canaan (*cf.* 7:2ff.). The identification of God's kingdom with the earthly kingdom of Israel brought an Old Testament anticipation of the final judgment which is to overtake those who remain outside the redemptive kingdom of Christ. This Old Testament judgment, however, could not be executed universally. For then the age of grace for the nations would have been prematurely terminated and the covenant promise that Israel should be a blessing to all the nations through the messianic seed of Abraham (*cf.* Gen. 12:3) would have been nullified.

Therefore, the typology of final judgment was strictly applied only in warfare against nations within the boundaries claimed by Yahweh for his typical kingdom (vv. 16-18; *cf.* 7:2ff.). *Thus shalt thou do unto all the cities which are very far off from thee, which are not of the cities of these nations* (v. 15). Beyond the boundaries of the theocracy the typology of judgment was tempered by the principles that govern the customary relations of ordinary nations (vv. 10-15), yet not so that the religious significance of the encounter of an ancient nation with God's kingdom Israel was lost. Consequently, in Israel's offer of peace (v. 10) and in the submission of the Gentile city as a covenant tributary to Yahweh (v. 11) there was imaged the saving mission of God's people in this world (*cf.* Zech. 9:7b, 10b; Luke 10:5-16). The judgment of those who refuse to make their peace with God through Christ was exhibited in the siege, conquest, and punishment of the unsubmissive city (v. 13), even though, as observed above, this did not amount to a strict application of the *ḥērem* (ban) nor was it even as severe treatment as was customary in ancient warfare (vv. 14, 12, 20). The words of verse 19 which are placed in parenthesis by AV are obscure, but AV seems to capture the original thought at the end of the verse more successfully than ASV or RSV.

f. AUTHORITY OF SANCTUARY AND HOME, 21:1-23

This chapter concludes the commandments concerned with governmental authority. Since all such authority is an extension of the authority of the individual family head (*cf.* the fifth commandment), these final stipulations on this subject appropriately deal with the exercise of authority within the home. There are sanctions imposed to enforce this authority (vv. 18-21) and there are regulations to insure a just exercise of it (vv. 10-17). The opening verses prescribe judicial procedure in the case where penal justice cannot be satisfied because the identity of the offender is unknown (vv. 1-9). The provisions are such as to demonstrate further the orientation of all theocratic government to the sanctuary. Similarly, the closing stipulation insists that cultic-ceremonial law be respected in the administration of criminal law (vv. 22, 23). The theocratic altar and the theocratic court were two manifestations of the justice of the theocratic King, the holy One who chose a dwelling place in Israel.

21:1-9. *If one be found slain . . . the city which is nearest unto the slain man* (vv. 1, 3, ASV). This principle of corporate community responsibility appears in cases of undetected criminals in the Code of Hammurapi also. Laws 23 and 24 of that code require the nearest city to make restitution in cases of robbery and to compensate with one mina of silver the family of someone slain. *Thy elders and thy judges* (v. 2), the members of the local judiciaries (*cf.* 16:18), determined which city must bear the responsibility, and then *the elders of that city* (v. 3a; *cf.* 19:12) as the representatives of the whole population were to conduct the ceremonial execution (vv. 3b, 4). This ritual was to be under the jurisdiction of *the priests* (v. 5a). *By their word shall every controversy and every stroke be tried* (v. 5b; *cf.* 17:8, 10). Here is a clear affirmation of the ultimate judicial authority vested in the priesthood. The priests' function in the case at hand was purely judicial, for the slaying of the heifer (v. 4b) was not a cultic sacrifice but a judicial execution. That it was not an altar sacrifice is evident from the mode of execution (*cf.* Ex. 13:13). Since it was only a ceremonial execution, with the heifer regarded as a substitute for the unknown murderer, there was no actual satisfaction of justice. *So shalt thou put away the innocent blood from the midst of thee* (v. 9, ASV). The ritual served to preserve the ceremonial status of those involved as sacramentally qualified covenant members (vv. 8, 9). In so doing, it prophetically prefigured (as would an altar sacrifice) the vicarious execution of the messianic Servant of the Lord for the blood-guiltiness of his people. Not only men, but the blood-stained land participated in the symbolical defilement, and its defilement, too, was, after a figure, purged by the judicial ritual (*cf.* Num. 35:33). In this there was a reminder that perfect righteousness must at last pervade the totality of God's kingdom. Another by-product of this ritual requirement would be the preservation of peace by the elimination of possible misunderstanding that might spark inter-city strife if the kinsman of the slain were rashly to pursue his role of avenger.

21:10-14. This first of three stipulations concerned with the authority of the head of the household (*cf.* vv. 15-21) deals with the limits of the husband's authority over his wife. The case of a captive woman (vv. 10, 11; *cf.* 20:14; contrast 7:3) is used as case in point for establishing the rights of the wife, perhaps because the principle would obviously apply *a fortiori* in the case of an Israelite wife. On the purificatory acts of verses 12b, 13a, which signified removal from captive-slave status, compare Leviticus 14:8; Numbers 8:7. On the month's mourning, see Numbers 20:29; Deuteronomy 34:8. This period would provide for the achieving of inward composure for beginning a new life, as well as for an appropriate expression of filial piety. *Thou shalt not sell her at all for money* (v. 14). A wife might not be reduced to slave status, not even the wife who had been raised from slave status. Though the particular illustration of the captive wife is peculiar to Deuteronomy, the same principle is expressed in the Book of the Covenant where the case of the Israelite bondmaiden is cited (Ex. 21:7-11). *If thou have no delight in her, then thou shalt let her go whither she will* (v. 14a). The severance of the marriage relationship is mentioned here only incidentally to the statement of the main principle that a man's authority did not extend to the right of reducing his wife to a slave (v. 14b). The dissolution of the marriage would have to be accomplished according to the laws of divorce in the theocracy (*cf.* 24:1-4). Not the divorce was mandatory but the granting of freedom in case the man should determine to divorce his wife according to the permission granted by Moses because of the hardness of their hearts (*cf.* Matt. 19:8).

21:15-17. This stipulation circumscribes the authority of the father over his sons, specifically with respect to the rights of the first-born. The particular illustration involves another situation which was merely tolerated within the Mosaic economy, namely, polygamy. Where polygamy was practiced, the problem cited (v. 15) would be common (*cf.* Gen. 29:30ff.; I Sam. 1:4ff.). *He shall acknowledge the first-born* (v. 17, ASV). The right of primogeniture included a property inheritance share double that of other sons. The principle here enforced is that parental authority is not absolute. A father's mere personal preference did not justify disregard of the divinely sanctioned customary rights of those who were under his parental authority. Similarly in Babylonian and Assyrian laws, a father might not disinherit his son without legal process and good reason alleged.

21:18-21. If misuse of authority produced tyranny, disrespect for proper authority would produce anarchy, the very contradiction of the covenant order as a manifestation of Yahweh's lordship. Parental authority in particular had been ordained of God to represent divine authority and to be the cornerstone of all human government and societal order. Therefore, while it was necessary to protect those under the authority of a household head from the arbitrary abuse of his authority (vv. 10-17), it was also necessary to fortify that authority against the spirit of lawlessness in a generation of Belial (v. 20). It is here enforced by the ultimate sanctions of theocratic law. *If a man have a stubborn and rebellious son* (v. 18) . . . *the men of his city shall stone him* (v. 21; Ex. 21:15, 17; Lev. 20:9; Deut. 27:16). Chastening was the limit of the parents' own enforcement of their authority (v. 18). Beyond that, the judicial process must be conducted by the elders at the gate (v. 19), that is, by the local theocratic judicatory (*cf.* 16:18ff.).

21:22, 23. The preceding law had proceeded from parental to official judicial authority and had prescribed the death penalty. The present case takes the judicial process a step beyond the execution to the exposure of the corpse as a monitory, public proclamation of the satisfaction of justice. The principle being exemplified is that all theocratic law administration must operate in the service of covenant religion. *He that is hanged is accursed of God* (v. 23). The condemned will have been guilty of offenses declared accursed in the covenant sanctions. As one executed, he would visibly embody the curse of God poured out. And as a human carcass exposed to birds and beasts of prey (*cf.* II Sam. 21:10), the man hung on a tree was an expression of the ultimate in the curse of God on the fallen race (*cf., e.g.,* Rev. 19:17ff.). In this conclusion to the series of stipulations wherein God demands a perfect judicial righteousness and the satisfaction of every claim of justice, if need be through a vicarious sufferer, the New Testament believer finds himself reminded of him who was made a curse to redeem his people from the inexorable curse of the law (Gal. 3:13).

3. SANCTITY OF THE DIVINE ORDER, 22:1-25:19

Love for God requires reverence for the divine ordinances at the various levels of creation and in the various spheres of human activity. The covenant servant must respect the sanctity of the divine order in the spheres of nature (22:5-30 [Heb. 23:1]) and of the theocratic kingdom (23:1 [Heb. 23:2]-25:12). With the partial exception of the natural order, the area in view is that of the mutual relationships of the covenant servants. This whole section, therefore, is bounded by laws which clearly express the basic principle that the same loving regard must be shown for one's neighbor's interests as for one's own (22:1-4;

25:13-16). The extra-biblical suzerainty treaties also regulated the relationships of the lord's vassals with one another.

a. THE REALM OF NATURE, 22:1-30

The stipulations under this heading are concerned with man's activity in the area of two of the creation ordinances. For man's relationship to the natural world (apart from his fellow man), which is the subject in 22:5-12, is governed by the creation ordinance of labor; and man's relationship to the human race in its genealogical history, which is dealt with in 22:5-30, is regulated by the creation ordinance of marriage.

22:1-4. Similar legislation is found in the Book of the Covenant (Ex. 23:4ff.). There it is in the midst of laws aimed at securing an honest administration of justice. The law of God must be obeyed by a man even in his secret actions which are beyond the detection of God's human agents of law enforcement. Deuteronomy 22:1-4 might thus well serve as an appendix to the preceding section on the enforcement of theocratic law. The reminder is provided that God's requirements concerning our relations with our neighbor are truly fulfilled only where there is a spirit of love that goes beyond mere concern for a technical legality sufficient to avoid the penal sanctions of human judiciaries and positively seeks the welfare of others as though it were our own. This law of love is the essential principle which the following stipulations apply in the particular life situations of the covenant people.

22:5-12. The Ordinance of Labor. Man must be mindful that in all the use he makes of this world he is God's steward. Various regulations were therefore prescribed for the Israelites which would continually remind them as they pursued the cultural program of God's kingdom (cf. Gen. 1:28) that the world is the Lord's, for he is its Maker. Man was indeed set as king over the earth with the whole order of nature under his dominion; but man's rule is a vicegerency in the Creator's name. Human authority must therefore be exercised according to the pattern God appoints. It is this fundamental principle which underlies the opening requirement of this section that the distinction between man and woman should not be blurred by the one appropriating the characteristic articles of the other (v. 5). God created them male and female with distinctive natures and functions; specifically, in the divinely established order of authority man is the head of the woman as together they reign over the earth. The Lord created the various "kinds" in the vegetable and animal kingdom (Gen. 1:11ff.). Israel was so to treat these "kinds" that they would be preserved in their distinctive natures (vv. 6, 7, 9-11; cf. Lev. 19:19). *That thou bring not blood upon thy house* (v. 8). Of special significance in the natural order of creation is the lifeblood of man. Carelessness with regard to it shows a want of neighborly love, and disrespect towards God. Guilt therefore is incurred before the Creator (v. 8), even though accidents resulting from such carelessness receive no human redress. *You shall make yourselves tassels on the four corners of your cloak* (v. 12, RSV). Like the other stipulations in this section the final regulation, requiring the appending of tassels to the outer garment, is designed to provide a special reminder of God's suzerainty over Israel (*cf.* Num. 15:37-41).

22:13-30. The Ordinance of Marriage. The sanctity of the divine institution of the family is the interest of the present provisions. *If any man takes a wife* (v. 13) . . . *and brings an evil name upon her* (v. 14, RSV). Verses 13-21 concern the allegation of unchastity brought by a husband against his bride, whether falsely (vv. 13-19) or justly (vv. 20, 21). In the first case, the malicious accuser was to suffer corporal punishment (v. 18; *cf.* 25:1-3), pay a compensation to his father-in-law for defaming his house (v. 19a), and retain his wife without ever being permitted to divorce her (v. 19b). In the second case, the guilty bride who had "wrought folly" was to suffer death by stoning before the disgraced house of her father. In societies where such evidence was legally decisive, it was customary after the marriage consummation to keep the tokens of the bride's virginity (v. 17). On the judicial responsibility of the elders (v. 17), *cf.* 19:12; 21:2-6, 19, 20; 25:7-9. On adultery, punishable by death (v. 22; *cf.* 5:18), *cf.* Leviticus 18:20, 29; 20:10.

Verses 23-29 concern the seduction of unmarried girls, whether betrothed (vv. 23-27) or unbetrothed (vv. 28, 29). If the girl was betrothed, the apprehended man was to be stoned to death. The same penalty befell the girl if their sexual intercourse occurred in the city (vv. 23, 24), but not if the circumstances permitted the reasonable assumption that she had been forced (vv. 25-27). The seducer of an unbetrothed virgin was obliged to take her as wife, paying the customary bride price and forfeiting the right of divorce. Probably the father's rights mentioned in Exodus 22:17 continued to have precedence. On verse 30, *cf.* Leviticus 18:6ff. and 20:11ff.; Deuteronomy 27:20ff. This single prohibition represents, as it recalls, the whole list of forbidden degrees of affinity.

b. THE THEOCRATIC KINGDOM, 23:1-25:19

The theme of these chapters is the sanctification of the theocratic kingdom. Israel must respect the sanctity of the congregation of the Lord as such (23:1-18 [Heb. 2-19]); the sanctity of special classes of God's servants, particularly the needy (23:19 [Heb. 20]-24:22); and the sanctity of every citizen of the theocracy as an individual bearer of God's image (25:1-12).

23:1-18. *The Sanctity of the Congregation of the Lord.* Israel was alerted to the sanctity of Yahweh's congregation by special stipulations governing access to congregational privilege (vv. 1-8 and vv. 15-18). The congregation's sacred character extended to Israel assembled as a military camp (vv. 9-14).

23:1-8. *Shall not enter into the congregation of the Lord* (vv. 1, 2, 3). The sacredness of the congregation of the Lord was signified by the exclusion from participation in the official theocratic assembly of those disqualified in various ways. The disqualification might be physical (vv. 1, 2) or ethnic and historical (vv. 3-8). The eunuch and the bastard, together with their descendants to the tenth generation (*i.e.*, indefinitely, *cf.* "for ever" in verse 3), were excluded (vv. 1, 2). The eunuch's condition was a mutilation of the divinely given nature (*cf.* 14:1). The bastard was the issue of a repudiation of the divinely appointed ordinance. Possibly the *mamzēr*, translated "bastard," was more precisely one born of an incestuous union (*cf.* 22:30). Such exclusions from covenant privilege point to the importance in covenant administration of the marriage design of securing a godly seed. Nevertheless, even in Old Testament days such physical disability was an obstacle only to external privilege, not to the spiritual realities of salvation. In New Testament times such disabilities no longer enter consideration even in the external administration of the church (*cf.* Isa. 56:4, 5; Acts 8:27, 28). The same is true of the cases of disqualification mentioned in verses 3-8.

Although the Ammonites and Moabites were begotten in incest (*cf.* v. 2; Gen. 19:30ff.), the reason assigned for their debarment is that they were unwilling to show hospitality to the people of God en route through the wilderness from Egypt to their homeland (v. 4a; *cf.* 2:18ff., 29) and even attempted offensive action against Israel: *They hired against thee Balaam the son of Beor of Pethor of Mesopotamia, to curse thee* (v. 4b; *cf.* Num. 22-25). The divine curse is the portion of those who would curse the covenant people, according to God's promise to Abraham (Gen. 12:3). Hence, theocratic Israel might not enter into covenantal alliance with these accursed would-be cursers (v. 6). In the case of the Edomites and Egyptians (vv. 7, 8), exclusion was again the rule because of their past enmity (*cf.* the Egyptian oppression, Ex. 1:8ff., and Edomite opposition, Num. 20:18ff.), but it was limited (*cf.* Ex. 20:5) because of ties of Abrahamic kinship (*cf.* Gen. 36:1ff.) or hospitality shown to Abraham's and Jacob's families when distressed by famine (Gen. 12:10ff.; 42:1ff.).

23:9-14. *Thou shalt keep thee from every evil thing* (v. 9, ASV). The military camp of Israel engaged in the wars of the Lord was an extension of the theocratic kingdom and must be characterized by that same sanctity which marked the settled covenant community. *For the Lord thy God walketh in the midst of thy camp* (v. 14). In war as in peace, God was present among his people and his name must be hallowed. Physical cleanliness was the appropriate symbol of the holiness of the covenant relationship. On verses 10, 11, *cf.* Leviticus 15:16.

23:15-18. These verses present further examples of what might or might not be deemed compatible with participation in the sacred congregation of the Lord. *Thou shalt not deliver unto his master the servant which is escaped from his master unto thee* (v. 15). This law relates to foreign runaway slaves. On the giving of asylum to the refugee, compare the extradition laws which are found in the secular treaties. *There shall be no whore . . . nor a sodomite* (v. 17). Female and male cultic prostitutes are meant as is suggested by the Hebrew terms, which are the feminine and masculine forms of a word whose root meaning is "sacred." The proscription is against native Israelites devoted to the abominable rites of pagan fertility cults. Verse 18 warns that the holy demands of God's covenant could not be satisfied by hiding sin under hypocritical piety. On *dog*, another term for a male prostitute, see Revelation 22:15. Lest the rules given in verses 3-8 leave the false impression that ethnic considerations were paramount, it was made clear by these two further rules in verses 15-18, the one welcoming the foreigner and the other excluding certain Israelites, that mercy and morality were the vital principles of covenant administration.

23:19-24:22. The Sanctity of the Lord's Servants. Respect was to be shown to all those dignified by the status of covenant servant to Yahweh. This section of stipulations would guarantee this sanctity of the theocratic citizen by regulations which assured peace, prosperity, and liberty within the covenant commitment to all God's people, but especially to those classes whose welfare was jeopardized by various circumstances. The legislation seems to be arranged in groups corresponding to laws six through ten in the Decalogue but in a slightly different order, as follows: laws of property (23: 19-25), of family (24:1-5), of life (24:6-15), of justice (24:16-18), and of charity (24:19-22).

23:19-25. Laws of Property. *Thou shalt not lend upon usury to thy brother* (v. 19). Impoverished Israelites were protected from exploitation at the hands of their richer brethren by the prohibition of interest on loans granted to them (*cf.* Ex. 22:25; Lev. 25:35ff.; Deut. 15:1ff.). Interest might be exacted from foreigners, however, because the loans made to them would not be for the relief of destitution but for business capital to be employed by these traveling merchants for profitable enterprise (v. 20). *If thou shalt forbear to vow, it shall be no sin in thee* (v. 22). Beyond the specified tributary demands of the covenant Lord, the property of the vassal was at his own disposal. This right was not intended, however, to discourage the free expression of religious love and gratitude, nor did it provide escape from the obligation of a voluntary vow once made. Reverencing his own holy name, God would not encourage a sense of carelessness or impunity in those who made solemn commitments to him (vv. 21, 23; *cf.* Lev. 27; Num. 30:2ff.). The law of crops (vv. 24, 25) provided such liberty as to satisfy the principle of brotherly hospitality but prohibited the changing of liberty to license in violation of the property rights of the theocratic citizen.

24:1-5. Laws of Family. Divorce as permitted in the Mosaic law (*cf.* Lev. 21:7, 14; 22:13; Num. 30:9) because of the hardness of the Israelites' hearts (Matt. 19:8; Mark 10:5) endangered the dignity of women within the theocracy. Hence, easy abuse of the permission was forestalled by circumscribing it with technicalities and restrictions (vv. 1-4). The RSV is correct in regarding verses 1-4 as one sentence, with verses 1-3 the condition and verse 4 the conclusion. The AV is liable to the interpretation that divorce was mandatory in the situation described. Actually, what was mandatory was not divorce, but (if divorce was resorted to) a legal process which included these elements: (a) A serious cause for the divorce. The exact import of the words *some uncleanness* (v. 1; *cf.* 23:14) is uncertain. Adultery is not meant, for the law prescribed the death penalty for that (22:13ff.; Lev. 20:10; *cf.* Num. 5:11ff.). (b) A writ of separation to be placed in the woman's hand for her subsequent protection. The preparation of this legal instrument implies the involvement of (c) a public official who might also have to judge of the adequacy of the alleged grounds of divorce. (d) A formal dismissal. *Her former husband, which sent her away, may not take her again to be his wife* (v. 4). The main point of the law is stated here in its conclusion. A man might not remarry his wife after he divorced her if she had meanwhile remarried, even though her second husband had divorced her or had died. With respect to the first husband the remarried divorcee was *defiled* (v. 4), such was the abnormality of this situation, tolerated in Old Testament times but abrogated by our Lord in the interests of the original standard (Matt. 19:9; Mark 10:6-9; *cf.* Gen. 2:23, 24). *When a man hath taken a new wife . . . he shall be free at home one year* (v. 5). Further respect was shown for the sanctity of the family relationship and especially for the welfare of the woman within it by granting a year's exemption from public services to the newly married man, that his bride might be gladdened by his presence.

24:6-15. Laws of Life. The concern of these stipulations is the life of God's people and things essential to the preservation of their life. Safeguards are afforded to the dignity and peace of the needy in particular, for the Lord delights to be the Help of the helpless and would have his people to be of like mind. *If a man be found stealing any of his brethren* (v. 7). Traffic in human life was forbidden under penalty of death (*cf.* Ex. 21:16). Men were not to be deprived of articles indispensable to life and health. In this category were the *millstone* (v. 6); the quadrangular mantle, used as a cover in sleeping (vv. 10-13; *cf.* Ex. 22:26, 27); and the day laborer's wages (vv. 14, 15; *cf.* Lev. 19:13). *When you make your neighbor a loan* (v. 10, RSV). Though interest on loans to Israelite neighbors was forbidden (23:19, 20), a pledge might be taken as security; but even this was not to be acquired in such a way as to prejudice the dignity (vv. 10, 11), let alone the life, of the debtor. *Lest he cry against thee unto the Lord* (v. 15). In the secular suzerainty treaties, too, complaints of one vassal against another were to be adjudicated by the suzerain. Respect for the whole community's life and health demanded careful attention to the divine prescriptions for dealing with the disease of leprosy (v. 8; *cf.* Lev. 13 and 14), the seriousness of which was evidenced by Miriam's experience (v. 9; *cf.* Num. 12:10ff.).

24:16-18. Laws of Justice. Justice must be dispensed to each Israelite in accordance with truth. *Every man shall be put to death for his own sin* (v. 16). The guilty individual alone was to be punished, not innocent members of his family (*cf.* II Kgs. 14:6). There is no contradiction between this and the divine judgment as described in the Decalogue (5:9; Ex. 20:5), for the latter does not say that God afflicts the innocent. Those who share in the visitation of judgment upon the fathers' iniquities are such as share also in the fathers' hatred of God. On the other hand, there is no repudiation of the principle of the corporate responsibility which obtains in certain group situations. *The stranger . . . the fatherless . . . a widow* (v. 17). Even the most helpless classes were to enjoy justice and be guaranteed all their legal rights. On the familiar appeal to the exodus (v. 18), *cf.* v. 22; 15:15.

24:19-22. Laws of Charity. *When thou reapest thy harvest* (v. 19). The spirit of charity, negatively required in the tenth commandment, was to be the governing spirit of theocratic life. Once again it is the poor who would be the beneficiaries. *Cf.* Leviticus 19:9f.; 23:22.

Chapter 25. Verses 1-12, the final laws on the sanctification of the kingdom (23:1 — 25:12), guard the sanctity of man as individual image-bearer of God. Then verses 13-19 conclude the entire section of laws on the sanctity of the divine order (chaps. 22-25), as they began (*cf.* 22:1-4), with the golden rule principle.

25:1-12. The Sanctity of God's Image-Bearer. The just punishment of the guilty was to be dispensed in such a way that his individual human dignity was honored (vv. 1-3). The principle of the sanctity of the individual God-like creature was thus enforced at the point where such respect might most plausibly seem to have been forfeited. Contrary to the sentence division in AV, the conclusion does not begin until verse 2 (so RSV). Unbecoming public degradation was to be prevented by several precautionary measures. The punishment of the criminal must be preceded by a trial and sentence, and it must be personally supervised by the judge. *Forty stripes he may give him, and not exceed: lest . . . thy brother should seem vile to thee* (v. 3). The stripes were to be scrupulously counted and not applied at random as to an animal or with the abandon of anger, unmindful that the judgment was the Lord's. The severity of the scourging was to be proportionate to the gravity of the offense, yet in no case to exceed forty stripes. *You shall not muzzle an ox when it treads out the grain* (v. 4, RSV). The positive counterpart to the prohibition of dishonoring a man in spite of his evil works is the requirement that he receive all proper honor for his good works. This verse, probably a proverbial expression, seems even here to have the force given it by Paul in I Corinthians 9:9 and I Timothy 5:18.

The covenant servant is an immortal being with a stake, even beyond death and the grave, in that future blessedness of God's kingdom which was promised in the Covenant of Redemption to believers and their seed after them (vv. 5-10). *That his name be not blotted out of Israel* (v. 6, ASV). Witness was to be borne to the dignity of the immortal servant-son of God by the perpetuation of his name in a covenant seed dwelling in his inheritance within the Old Testament typical kingdom. As an application of this the Deuteronomic Covenant adopted a form of the widespread practice of levirate marriage, whereby there devolved upon the brother of a man who died childless the duty of raising up an heir to the dead by his widow (v. 6). This requirement constituted an exception to the prohibition in Leviticus 18:16; 20:21. For biblical examples of this or similar practice, see Genesis 38 and the Book of Ruth. The levirate duty is limited in Deuteronomy to situations where brothers shared the same estate (v. 5a), and even then it was not compulsory (v. 7). Failure to comply, however, betrayed a want of fraternal affection and was publicly stigmatized (vv. 8-10). On the transfer of the sandal for confirming legal transfer of right of property, *cf.* Ruth 4:7. In view of the provision of Numbers 27:4ff., there would be no need for the levirate marriage if the deceased had daughters. Hence the AV seems preferable to RSV in rendering in verse 5 *no child*, rather than *no son*.

Verses 11, 12 are also concerned with the dignity of the individual and indeed precisely with his dignity as God's covenant servant who in his circumcision bears in his body the

sign of the covenant. The reference to the organ of repro-
duction might account for the immediate conjunction of this
prohibition with the law of levirate marriage. That the act
forbidden includes contempt for the covenant sign and not
just indecency is suggested by the apparent similarity in the
nature of the punishment and the sign, both involving a mutilation of the body. This is the more significant since apart from
this case only the *lex talionis* (19:21) calls for such penal
mutilation.

25:13-19. *Thou shalt have a perfect and just weight* (v. 15).
Neighbor must be loved as self (vv. 13-16); therefore, business
with one's neighbor was not to be conducted with two sets of
measuring standards, the large for receiving, the small for dis-
pensing (*cf.* Amos 8:5). This law somewhat expands Leviticus
19:35, 36, especially by the appended blessings and curses of
the covenant. While this law of love sums up the requirements
for inter-theocratic relationships dealt with in the immediately
preceding sections of stipulations, no repudiation of the mandate
of conquest (*cf.* Deut. 7; 20:16, 17) is intended (see 25:17-19).
Nor is there any contradiction between the two. For though
God requires love of neighbor, those who set themselves to
destroy the people of the typical, Old Testament theocratic
kingdom removed themselves from the neighbor category,
just as those doomed with Satan in eternal perdition are not the
neighbors of the inhabitants of the heavenly theocracy. On the
charge to exterminate Amalek, see Exodus 17:8-16. Taken together, the laws of love and hate amount to the single requirement to love God and, expressive of this love of God, to love
whom he loves and hate whom he hates.

4. CONFESSION OF GOD AS REDEEMER-KING, 26:1-19

The long stipulations division (chaps. 5-26) draws to a close
with the liturgies for two cultic confessions (vv. 1-11 and vv.
12-15) and a declaration of the ratification of the covenant (vv.
16-19).

26:1-11. *Thou shalt go unto the priest that shall be in those
days, and say unto him, I profess this day unto the Lord* (v. 3).
The Israelite servants of the covenant Lord were to make continual thankful acknowledgment that their goodly inheritance
in Canaan was the gift of his redemptive grace in fulfillment of
his oath to the patriarchs (v. 3). They were to confess his
continuing lordship and express their consecration by a tributary

offering of the firstfruits (vv. 2, 10). On the law of firstfruits, see 18:4; Exodus 23:19; 34:26; Numbers 18:12ff. Elements of firstfruit offering are found in connection with each of the annual feasts (*cf.* Deut. 16). For example, at the feast of Unleavened Bread a sheaf of firstfruits was waved (Lev. 23:10ff.). Also, the feast of Weeks was called "the day of firstfruits" (Num. 28:26; *cf.* Ex. 23:16; 34:22) and two firstfruit loaves were offered at it (Lev. 23:17); and the firstfruits of wine could not be offered until the feast of Tabernacles when the vintage had ripened. If *all the fruit of the ground* (v. 2) indicates the end of the harvest season, the feast of Tabernacles would be the occasion for the presentation of this basket of firstfruits at the central altar. Grammatically, verse 2 can be understood as describing all the firstfruits of the ground or only a token basket thereof. In the case of agricultural firstfruits, the amount is nowhere specified. Since firstfruits were assigned to the priests (Num. 18:13, 14), the reference to the sacred feast which the offerer was to enjoy after this ritual (v. 11; *cf.* 12:6f., 11f., 17f.; 16:11, 14) would indicate that the basket represented only a token of the firstfruits (see comments on 14:22ff.; 15:20), at least if this feast was provisioned out of the firstfruits. That, however, is uncertain.

The Israelite must confess that the theocratic calling of his people could not be attributed to their might (vv. 5ff.; *cf.* 7:7, 8; 8:17, 18). *A wandering Aramean was my father* (v. 5b, RSV). The Hebrew *'ōbēd* connotes the ideas of "lost" and "in peril"; *cf.* "ready to perish" (AV). The reference is to Jacob. He is called *Aramean* because the patriarchal origins were geographically, though not racially, Aramean and because Jacob himself sojourned in Aram-naharaim during the period of the birth of his sons, the future tribal fathers of Israel. The commemorative recital of God's redemptive acts in exodus and conquest (vv. 7-9) was Israel's confessional Amen to God's own recital of his favor to them in the historical prologue of the covenant. Verse 10b does not describe a chronologically successive step in the ritual (in contradiction of verse 4); it is rather a summarizing conclusion.

26:12-15. The dependence of Israel on the Lord for continuing prosperity was to be expressed in a special triennial service of petition for his favorable attention and blessing. On the tithing regulations, see the comments on 14:22ff. *Before the Lord thy God* (v. 13); this probably refers to the central sanctuary. If so, then the emphasis on the completion of the tithing process (vv. 12, 13) suggests that the feast of Tabernacles was the occasion. Perhaps this liturgy followed immediately upon that of the presentation of the basket of firstfruits (vv. 1-11). *I have brought away the hallowed things out of mine house* (v. 13) . . . *Look down from thy holy habitation, from heaven, and bless thy people Israel* (v. 15). The avowal of obedience to all the tithing prescriptions (vv. 13, 14) as the preliminary to the petition for divine blessing (v. 15) recalls the fact that God declared the latter to be contingent on the former (14:28, 29). The worshiper must affirm that his tithe had not been exposed to ceremonial defilement, particularly, the uncleanness associated with mourning for the dead (v. 14; *cf.* Lev. 22:3ff.; Num. 19:11ff.; Hos. 9:4).

26:16-19. The central act in the ceremony of covenant ratification was the oath of allegiance which the vassal took to his lord in response to the declaration of the covenant stipulations and sanctions. Israel took such an oath after the reading of the Book of the Covenant at Sinai (Ex. 24:7) and now Israel must do the same in the plains of Moab, as is reflected in these verses (see also 29:10-15). The Lord demands covenantal consecration (v. 16). *Thou hast avouched the Lord this day to be thy God* (v. 17). Israel avows that they submit to Yahweh as their God to be obeyed according to all his holy will. *And the Lord hath avouched thee this day to be his peculiar people* (v. 18). The Lord graciously acknowledges them as his people, and guarantees the blessings of the covenant to the faithful (vv. 18b, 19; *cf.* 7:6; 14:2; Ex. 19:5, 6).

IV. SANCTIONS: COVENANT RATIFICATION, 27:1-30:20

The fourth standard division in the Near Eastern suzerainty treaties was the curses and blessings, the woe and weal sanctions of the covenant. In Deuteronomy this section is found in chapters 27-30. While 26:16-19 forms a conclusion to the stipulations, it also introduces the element of covenant ratification, the nucleus around which the curses and blessings of these chapters cluster. The ratification of the new covenant which Moses was making with the second generation was to unfold in two stages. That was customary procedure in securing the throne succession to the appointed royal heir. When death was imminent, the suzerain required his vassals to pledge obedience to his son; then, soon after the son's accession, the vassals' commitment was repeated. Similarly, Moses and Joshua formed a dynasty of royal mediatorial representatives of Yahweh's suzerainty over Israel. Hence the succession of Joshua, which symbolized the continuing lordship of Yahweh, was ensured by the oath elicited from Israel before Moses died, and again later by a ratificatory ceremony after Joshua's accession. The pronouncing of curses and blessings is prominent in each of these ratification rituals.

The sanctions section of Deuteronomy opens with the curses and blessings to be used at the second stage of the ratification (chap. 27), then returns to the initial stage of ratification and its solemn sanctions (chaps. 28-30). When Deuteronomy is considered as the finished legal documentary witness to the covenant, no difficulty need be felt with the position assigned to the directions of chapter 27. On the other hand, the connection between the end of chapter 26 and the beginning of chapter 28 is so smooth as to suggest the possibility that chapter 27 may not have intervened at this precise point in the progress of the ceremony in Moab. Similarly, in the original flow of Moses' oration Deuteronomy 30 might have followed immediately upon the end of chapter 28.

A. RATIFICATION CEREMONY IN CANAAN, 27:1-26

Moses prescribes the ceremony for the second stage of the covenant renewal, to be conducted in Canaan (vv. 1-8). The

121

re-establishment of the covenant is proclaimed (vv. 9, 10). A charge is given concerning the recital of blessings and curses in the later ceremony (vv. 11-26). For the historical performance of what is here prescribed, see Joshua 8:30-35. For an anticipation of these instructions among the Deuteronomic stipulations, see Deuteronomy 11:26-30.

27:1-8. To promote respect for the appointed authorities, Moses associated with himself in this solemn hour Israel's elders (v. 1) and priests (*cf.* v. 9). The time of the final ratification was to be after Moses' death when Israel under Joshua was in Canaan (v. 2a). Its setting was to be the impressive one of the adjacent mountains, Ebal and Gerizim, between which lay Shechem (v. 4; *cf.* vv. 12, 13). There is no record of a military effort having been necessary to take that area of Canaan. The essential element of the ceremony would be Israel's self-consecration to the covenant Lord. The burnt-offerings (v. 6) symbolized such consecration. To similar effect was the series of self-maledictory oaths (*cf.* vv. 15ff.).

Thou shalt set thee up great stones, and plaister them with plaister: And thou shalt write upon them all the words of this law (vv. 2, 3). Covenant consecration must be an act of intelligent, informed faith and devotion. Therefore, the content of the covenant was to be published preparatory to its ratification by the people. That was one purpose of writing the covenant on the plastered stones (an Egyptian technique), as is confirmed by the fact that in the historical fulfillment Joshua read this law to the people (Josh. 8:34). Comparable were Moses' reading of the Book of the Covenant to Israel at the ratification of the Sinaitic Covenant and the proclamation of the Deuteronomic Covenant in the plains of Moab. The fact that durable stones were to be selected invites comparison with the two stone tables of the law written by the finger of God and suggests that a further purpose was to provide a symbolic witness to the permanence of the covenant (*cf.* 31:26; Josh. 24:26, 27). *All the words of this law* (v. 3). This refers to the Deuteronomic Covenant, *law* being used *pars pro toto*. The ceremonial feast was another recognized symbolic method by which people ratified treaties. That is the significance of the peace-offerings and the associated joyous meal (v. 7; *cf.* Ex. 24:11).

There thou shalt build an altar unto the Lord (v. 5). For the purpose of the sacrificial offerings, a special altar was to be erected on Ebal. It may be that the mount of cursing was selected because the Mosaic economy was in its distinctive emphasis as a schoolmaster conducting to the grace of Christ a ministration of death and condemnation (*cf.* II Cor. 3:7-9). Or possibly the altar was to be erected on Ebal because the peaçe of the covenant was to come through the infliction of the curses on the Redeemer-Servant, sacrificed for the sins of God's people. The altar was to be made of unhewn stones in accordance with the requirement of the Book of the Covenant (Ex. 20:25). Clearly .he Deuteronomic law of the permanent central altar was not intended to be a repudiation of the altar law of the Book of the Covenant. Nor was the principle of the centralization of the altar so absolutely restrictive that there might not be the special altar for extraordinary occasions (*cf.* comments on 12:4-14).

27:9, 10. In the midst of the instructions concerned with the later stage in the renewal process a solemn reminder is given that the covenantal engagement has already, on this day of the Deuteronomic proclamation, been entered upon.

27:11-26. Six tribes descending from Jacob's wives Leah and Rachel were to stand on the slopes of the mount of blessing and two of similar descent — the tribe of Reuben, who forfeited the birthright by the sin of incest (Gen. 49:4; *cf.* Deut. 27:20), and the tribe of Zebulun, Leah's youngest son — were to join the four tribes descending from the handmaids on the mount of cursing (vv. 12, 13). Whether the two sets of tribes were to fulfill their respective roles unto curse and blessing simply by having either curse or blessing formulae directed toward them, or by themselves reciting or at least assenting to one or the other is not stated. In chapter 28 there appear matching sets of six blessings (vv. 3-6) and six curses (vv. 16-19); it seems difficult to dissociate these from the present two sets of six tribes. Deuteronomy 28, as part of the entire renewal treaty, will have been read by Joshua before all the assembly of Israel (*cf.* Josh. 8:34, 35).

The Levites shall speak, and say unto all the men of Israel with a loud voice (v. 14). Here *Levites* refers to the priests (*cf.* 31:25; 33:8-10). They were to be stationed with the ark of the covenant between Ebal and Gerizim (*cf.* Josh. 8:33) to lead Israel in the oath of ratification. This oath consisted in a series of twelve self-maledictions (vv. 15-26). The repeated *cursed be* identifies the covenant-breaker's fate with that of the serpent (*cf.* Gen. 3:14). The *Amen* response was the customary formula of assent (*cf.* Num. 5:22; I Kgs. 1:36; Neh. 5:13; 8:6;

Ps. 72:19). The fact that only curses and not blessings are given in verses 15ff. indicates that this is not the detailed account of the curse and blessing proclamation by the two pairs of six tribes mentioned in verses 12, 13. A similar indication is the fact that verses 15ff. were to be addressed to and receive response from all the Israelites (v. 14). This section rather describes a separate feature of the covenant ceremony, the actual oath, which characteristically took the form of provisional self-maledictions, but not benedictions. In contrast to the curses in chapter 28, the several members of this series differ not in variety of curse but in kind of sin. The area of transgression covered is that of secret sins likely to escape human detection and punishment (note especially vv. 15, 24; cf. Job 31:24ff.) and, therefore, peculiarly the judicial province of God as divine Witness to the oath. They are imprecated who secretly violate God's demands for respect to himself (v. 15), to rightful authority (v. 16), to truth (vv. 17-19), to family (vv. 20-23), to human life (vv. 24, 25), and in sum to God's covenant (v. 26).

B. BLESSINGS AND CURSES, 28:1-68

Returning to the first stage of the ceremony of covenant renewal, Moses pronounces its sanctions. In the corresponding section of the Sinaitic Book of the Covenant (Ex. 23:20-33), the blessings predominated. Now, the forty years history of Israelite apostasy having intervened, Moses' emphasis falls heavily on the curses; thus, blessings (vv. 1-14) and curses (vv. 15-68). This emphasis was anticipated in the promises and threats of a similar section in Leviticus (chap. 26), written after Israel's earliest rebellion against the Sinaitic Covenant. The remarkable preview in Deuteronomy 28-30 of Israel's history, especially of the far-off exile, has been a major stumblingblock to the recognition of the Mosaic origin of this document by naturalistic higher criticism.

28:1-14. Blessings. (Cf. 7:12ff.; 11:13ff., 22ff.) *If thou shalt hearken diligently unto the voice of the Lord thy God . . . the Lord thy God will set thee on high above all nations of the earth* (v. 1). Although Israel's inheritance and continued enjoyment of the promises was not a matter of legal merit, there was a connection between the nation's corporate piety and prosperity. For the Old Testament theocratic kingdom prefigured the consummate kingdom of God, in which righteousness and glory are united. Accordingly, to keep the typical-prophetic picture clear God allowed the Israelites to enjoy the blessings of the typical kingdom only as they, and especially their official representatives, exhibited an appropriate measure of the righteousness of the kingdom. Since any righteousness that Israel possessed was a gift of grace from the God of their salvation, the principle which informs Deuteronomy 28 has no affinities with a religion of works-salvation (see comments on 6:1-3). Verses 3-6 present six blessings which are paralleled by six curses in verses 16-19. On the apparent use of these at the later ceremony in Canaan, see comments on 27:12, 13. The blessings depict a comprehensive fullness of beatitude. The paired opposites, for example, express totality (vv. 3, 6).

What was concisely presented in liturgical formulae in the six beatitudes is elaborated in verses 7-14. The arrangement of the blessings is chiastic: thus, foreign relations (v. 7 and vv. 12b, 13); domestic affairs (v. 8 and vv. 11, 12a); and in the center position, relationship to the Lord (vv. 9, 10). Israel, if faithful to the covenant oath, would come out on top in every military and commercial encounter with other nations. Within the kingdom there would be abundance of the earth's goodness. Canaan would be a veritable paradise, flowing with milk and honey. Of primary import, Israel would prosper in her relationship to her covenant Lord. That is the secret of all beatitude, for his favor is life. From the manifest tokens of God's favor to Israel all the earth would recognize that *the name of the Lord is called upon thee* (v. 10). That is, it would be clear that God's covenant was established with Israel and that he, the covenant Suzerain, was Israel's Owner and Defender (*cf.* Isa. 63:19; Jer. 7:10, 11; 15:16). Once and again the prerequisite covenant loyalty is recalled (vv. 9b, 13b, 14).

28:15-68. Curses. Banishment from the promised inheritance was the extreme of malediction. It signified the loss of God's special presence and favor, loss of the appointed sacramental access to him on his holy hill of Zion, and loss of status as the people of God's kingdom. In this long section of curses, therefore, siege and exile repeatedly appear as the climax of woe. There is a series of parallel pictures of the disastrous future looming before this nation so prone to unfaithfulness: verses 20-26, 27-37, 38-48, 49-57, and 58-68. The first three and the last of these pictures culminate in the doom of conquest by the enemy, with its dreadful sequel (vv. 25f., 36f., 48, and

63-68); the fourth is completely devoted to that accursed event (vv. 49-57). This extended description of particular evils follows an introductory, ritualistic formulation of the covenant's curse sanctions (vv. 15-19).

28:15-19. Verse 15 corresponds to verses 1, 2 and verses 16-19 are the counterpart to verses 3-6. The vengeance of the covenant (cf. Lev. 26:25) would overtake the oath-violating people even within the asylum of their inherited paradise land. Without holiness no man can abide where God reveals his glorious presence and there is no respect of persons with him.

28:20-26. *Thou hast forsaken me* (v. 20). Such was the essence of Israel's sin — violation of the first commandment of the covenant. *The Lord will send* (v. 20). It was the right and duty of the forsaken Lord himself, the One to whom and by whom Israel swore the covenant oath, to avenge the oath. Whatever the human or earthly origin of the several curses, the Lord was their ultimate Author. *Until thou be destroyed* (v. 20; cf. vv. 24, 45, 51, 61). It is repeatedly stated here that the final issue of the various types of curses — epidemic (vv. 21, 22a), drought (vv. 22b-24), and war (vv. 25, 26) — would be nothing short of Israel's destruction (vv. 20, 21, 22, 24, 26). The dust-rain of verse 24 refers to the filling of the air with sand and dust by the sirocco. Verse 25 is the reversal of verse 7 (cf. Lev. 26:17). *And thy dead body shall be food unto all the birds of the heavens, and unto the beasts of the earth; and there shall be none to frighten them away* (v. 26, ASV). The curse principle is essentially the prostration of man under the sub-human realms over which God appointed him in the beginning as king. Hence, the Scripture depicts the doom of rebel mankind as an eschatological feast in which slain men are devoured by birds and beasts (cf. Ps. 79:2; Ezek. 39:4, 17ff.; Rev. 19:17, 18).

28:27-37. Vexation and frustration characterize the curses of this section. Observe the references in almost every verse to the utter impotence of the Israelites to cope with their afflictions, or to their helplessness in the face of oppression. God created man as one who, entering into the program of his kingdom, might rejoice to follow the divine sabbatic pattern of labor crowned with the joy and satisfaction of consummation. But accursed Israel's kingdom undertakings in the area of the creation ordinances of marriage and labor would be rewarded always and only with failure. Instead of attaining to the sabbath joy of accomplishment, the Israelites would be driven mad with the vanity and frustration of their exertions (vv. 28, 34). The contents of verses 27-35 are chiastically arranged: (a) incurable disease, v. 27; (b) madness, v. 28; (c) continual oppression, v. 29; (d) frustration, vv. 30-32; (c) continual oppression, v. 33; (b) madness, v. 34; (a) incurable disease, v. 35. The similarities to the calamities of Job are noteworthy.

The Lord shall bring thee, and thy king which thou shalt set over thee, unto a nation which neither thou nor thy fathers have known (v. 36a). The section ends with the curse of conquest by a foreign nation, which was anticipated in verses 32, 33. God would afflict the apostates by abandoning them to their own reprobate mind and worship of idols (v. 36; cf. v. 64; 4:27). *There shalt thou serve other gods, wood and stone* (v. 36b). In idolatry man substitutes a subservience to creatures beneath him for self-consecration to the Suzerain above him. In so doing he seals his own helplessness in sin; for, cutting himself off from the Lord-Protector, the Rock who delights to deliver the helpless, he looks in vain to a covenant lord weaker than himself. The essential nature of the curse principle once more finds expression in this worship rendered by man to the sub-human over which the Creator made him king. *Thou shalt become an astonishment, a proverb, and a byword* (v. 37). Israel, heir of the promise that all nations would be blessed in them, would become proverbially identified with cursedness by all peoples.

28:38-48. Here again the curse takes the form of failure and frustration (vv. 38-42), the opposite of the blessings of verses 8, 11ff. The crop pests, another sector of man's erstwhile total dominion (cf. Gen. 1:26), in effect make the Israelites their servants who must labor to feed them (vv. 38, 39). On verse 41, cf. verse 32. *Thou shalt come down very low* (v. 43) . . . *he shall be the head, and thou shalt be the tail* (v. 44). This is the reverse of the beatitude of verses 12b, 13. In verses 45-48 there is a summation of the preceding threats of curse, both as to cause (cf. v. 20) and as to result. *Because thou hearkenest not* (v. 45). The cause would be Israel's breaking of the covenant oath; the result would be that Israel would suffer the full vengeance of the covenant to the extremity of exile's devastation. *And upon thy seed forever* (v. 46b). If this threat means more than that the climactic Old Testament exile-judgment of Israel would serve as a perpetual sign of God's covenant vengeance, if a perpetual divine cursing of Israel is predicted, then Moses here warns of that which Paul declares to have become a fixed decree (I Thess. 2:16). *Because thou servedst not the Lord* (v. 47) . . . *therefore shalt thou serve thine enemies* (v. 48). The punishment fits the crime. *He shall put a yoke of iron upon thy neck* (v. 48). Israel's curse-yoke would amount to a return to the status from which God had called her in covenant love (*cf.* Lev. 26:13). Though Moses does not at this point detract from the impressiveness of these curses by any qualifications, elsewhere he proclaims the triumph of covenant grace through the restoration of an elect, repentant remnant (4:29ff.; 30:1ff.).

28:49-57. What had constituted the climax in each of the preceding series is the exclusive subject of this fourth prophetic picture of Israel, overtaken by the covenant curse. With unsparing vividness Moses exposes the appalling distress and degradation to which this people, once the head of the nations, would be reduced when caught in the curse of the siege. *The Lord shall bring a nation against thee from afar, from the end of the earth, as swift as the eagle flieth* (v. 49). The barbarian invader from afar, descending on Israel like a vulture on its prey (v. 49), would be unpitying in its rapacity (vv. 50, 51). But the inhumanity of the enemy warrior pales beside the bestiality of even the tenderest Israelite mother, turned cannibalistic in the horror of the siege (vv. 52-57; *cf.* Lev. 26:29; Lam. 4:1-10). *And he shall eat the fruit of thy cattle, and the fruit of thy land* (v. 51) . . . *And thou shalt eat the fruit of thine own body* (v. 53). The passage contrasts the natural appetite of the barbarian and the unnatural lust of the Israelites (vv. 53ff.). There is no refuge from the siege anywhere in the land (vv. 52, 55, 57) for those who have put their trust in human defenses rather than in God, their true Refuge (v. 52b). Old Testament history witnessed successive executions of this curse, and it was finally exhausted in the Fall of Jerusalem in 70 A.D.

28:58-68. *If thou wilt not observe to do all the words of this law that are written in this book* (v. 58). In this closing paragraph Moses harks back to the conditional form with which the pronouncing of the curses began (*cf.* v. 15), for in the day of assembly in Moab the decision between the curses and the blessings was still to be made by Israel. To avoid the curses Israel must obey the stipulations of this covenant document out of true reverence for the Lord who had revealed his glory and fearful works in saving them from Egypt. *Ye shall be left few*

in number (v. 62) . . . *Ye shall be plucked from off the land*
(v. 63). Disobedience would bring loss of those blessings which
were promised in the Abrahamic Covenant, namely, the multiplication of the people (vv. 62, 63a) and the possession of a
homeland (vv. 63ff.). In place of the blessings would be every
possible extraordinary and persistent affliction (vv. 59-61).
*The Lord shall scatter thee among all people, from the one end
of the earth even unto the other* (v. 64). Prophetically following the besieged and conquered people into their exile (vv. 64-
67), Moses catches with a few strokes all the pathos of unbelieving homeless Israel down through the centuries — once
the people of God, but become in their exile like unto the
heathen, without Christ, having no hope, without God in the
world (*cf.* Eph. 2:12). *The Lord shall bring thee into Egypt
again* (v. 68). By repudiating their election and covenant calling, in virtue of which they had been delivered from Egyptian
slavery to become God's theocratic sons, Israel would be doomed
to fall back into a worse Egyptian bondage, into bondage to
Satan and sin, death and hell.

C. SUMMONS TO THE COVENANT OATH, 29:1-29

In a direct, personal appeal to the generation standing before
him, Moses confronts them with the central purpose of the
ceremony of this great day (vv. 10-15). The central demand
for the oath of allegiance is preceded by a reminder of the
Lord's past works of salvation (vv. 2-9) and it is followed by a
warning that the curses of the covenant will be visited on an
unfaithful nation throughout their generations (vv. 16-29). This
section thus reflects the over-all pattern of the treaty.

29:1 [Hebrew 28:69]. *These are the words of the covenant,
which the Lord commanded Moses to make with the children
of Israel in the land of Moab, beside the covenant which he
made with them in Horeb* (v. 1). Though some, following the
Hebrew arrangement, regard this as a subscription, and it would
indeed be an accurate description of what preceded, it is
probably to be understood as a superscription. On the relation
of verses 1 and 2, compare the similar sequence from 4:45 to
5:1. There is essential continuity in God's Covenant of Redemption from Genesis through Revelation. Nevertheless, the
successive administrations of that Covenant, as it is repeatedly
renewed by divine grace, are to be distinguished. The covenant
in Moab renewed the covenant at Sinai, which renewed the

covenant with Abraham, which renewed the covenant with
Adam (*cf.* Gen. 3:15; Deut. 5:2, 3).

29:2-9. *I have led you forty years in the wilderness* (v. 5) ...
that ye might know that I am the Lord your God (v. 6).
The mercy and the miracle of the deliverance from Egypt and
the passage through the wilderness should have opened the eyes
of this generation to the supreme wisdom of giving themselves
in wholehearted love to so great and gracious a Lord (vv.
2, 3, 5-8). But the simplest spiritual knowledge is beyond the
perception of man the sinner except the Spirit of God grant
him understanding as a sovereign gift of grace: *Yet the Lord
hath not given you an heart to perceive* (v. 4). This people, so
signally favored as to have lived forty years in the atmosphere
of supernatural providence, lacked that necessary gift (*cf.* 9:7,
24). The responsibility for this spiritual dullness was Israel's and
by this reproof they are incited to a better response to their
Lord: *Keep therefore the words of this covenant* (v. 9). The
imperceptible way in which the appeal of Moses becomes in
verses 5, 6 the direct appeal of God evidences the reality of the
supernatural revelation which came through Moses, God's mediator (*cf.* 7:4; 11:15; 17:3; 28:20). On verses 5, 6, *cf.* 8:2ff.
On verses 7, 8, *cf.* 2:30ff.; 3:1ff.

29:10-15. *Ye stand this day all of you before the Lord your
God* (v. 10). The central act of covenant ratification and its
significance are here declared. The terms of verses 10, 11 suggest
the solemnly formal nature of the assembly and stress the
fact that the entire covenant community was present for participation in the oath. Women and children, non-Israelites (*cf.*
Ex. 12:38; Num. 10:29; 11:4), and servants (v. 11c; *cf.* Josh.
9:21) are included. *That thou shouldest enter into covenant
with the Lord* (v. 12). The Hebrew phrase, found only here,
means literally, "pass over into," or "pass through." According
to the latter translation, the expression might derive from a
ceremony of oath taking like that in Genesis 15:17, 18. *And
into his oath* (v. 12). The equation of the Lord's covenant with
the oath that he required of Israel (see, too, v. 14) is a significant index to the nature of the covenant as an instrument of
God's rule whereby he secures the commitment of a people to
his service. *That he may establish thee today for a people
unto himself, and that he may be unto thee a God* (v. 13). This
verse, too, speaks of the servant's consecration to the Lord, indicating at the same time that God's establishment of covenant

relationship with man is not a humiliating subjugation but an act of redemptive favor. It fulfills the promise and oath in which the children of God have found hope and consolation (v. 13b; cf. Heb. 6:17, 18). *And also with him that is not here with us this day* (v. 15b). This means that there is a genealogical continuity to the covenant. Such is the case not because salvation is an inalienable family heirloom but because God is faithful to his promise to extend his covenant mercies to the thousandth generation of those who love him and because covenant administration respects parental authority (vv. 14, 15). Accordingly, the covenant with its sacramental sign of consecration is administered to believers together with their children.

29:16-29. *For* (v. 16) and *lest* (v. 18) both assume some antecedent thought. The idea to be supplied is probably that of the call to faithful allegiance which was presented in the preceding section. Thus: (Remember, O Israel, that Yahweh is your God), *for*, as you well know, the temptation to idolatry comes to you from all the surrounding nations (vv. 16, 17). (Remember), *lest* idolatry take root among you and you reap a bitter, poisonous harvest (v. 18; cf. Heb. 12:15). The theme of Israel's peril, depicted under the figure of the root and the gall and wormwood in verse 18b, is developed in verses 19-28: the *root* in verses 19-21, and the ultimate bitter fruit in verses 22-28. *To the sweeping away of moist and dry alike* (v. 19b, RSV). The reference of this proverbial phrase is to plants; watered and thirsty plants means all plants. It continues the figure of verse 18b, warning again that if idolatry took hold in Israel, its ultimate issue must be deadly; indeed, it must be the ruin of the entire people. *Then the anger of the Lord and his jealousy shall smoke against that man* (v. 20). As for the root of the trouble, the individual who hypocritically mouthed the self-maledictory oath of the covenant (v. 19b), Yahweh would not hold him guiltless for having taken his name in vain. Though the individual think himself hidden in the assembled host of Israel and suppose his hypocrisy concealed within his own heart, Yahweh, avenging divine Witness of the oath, would single him out and mercilessly pour on him all the curses he had idly invoked. On verse 20b, cf. Revelation 22:18, 19. *The generation to come* (v. 22). Abruptly changing his standpoint to the future, to a time even beyond the threatened desolation of the theocracy and the exile (see v. 28), Moses depicts the fearful consequences that would at last befall the whole nation (vv. 22-28) for having forsaken the covenant by transferring their allegiance to idol god-kings (vv. 25, 26). He does so through the device of a dramatic dialogue between Israelites and foreigners standing amid the charred ruins of the theocratic land, a former paradise turned like the cities of the plain into a barren waste by the fury of God's judgment (v. 23). *Those things that are revealed belong unto us and to our children for ever* (v. 29). Attention to the Lord's revealed demand for consecration is the life business of his servants (*cf.* 30:11ff.), not lusting after knowledge of divine mysteries (*cf.* Gen. 3:5).

D. ULTIMATE RESTORATION, 30:1-10

Beyond the curse of exile opens the prospect of restoration (vv. 1-10; *cf.* 4:29-31; Lev. 26:40-45). The redemptive program does not fail in the fall of those who were of Israel yet were not Israel (*cf.* Rom. 9:6). A remnant out of Israel together with the remnant of the Gentiles are to be restored to the covenant Lord in his kingdom of glory. Of this ultimate restoration the Old Testament return from Babylonian exile was typical. The one vast complex of typical and antitypical restoration is embraced in this prophetic blessing of Moses.

30:1-10. *And it shall come to pass, when all these things are come upon thee, the blessing and the curse, which I have set before thee* (v. 1). In 28:64ff. Moses portrayed the hopelessness of unbelieving Israelites in their dispersion among the nations. Here again he looks beyond the exile, indeed, beyond all the curse and blessing described hitherto in these covenant sanctions and he now presents the hope of restoration, the hope of a new covenant. (*Thou*) *shalt return unto the Lord thy God* (v. 2). The way into this new beatitude would be the way of a re- newed and true consecration to the Lord against whom Israel had rebelled (*cf.* vv. 8, 10). *The Lord thy God will circumcise thine heart, and the heart of thy seed, to love the Lord thy God* (v. 6). The origin of that repentance and heart-love for the Lord would be in a divine work of qualification. What had been externally symbolized in circumcision, the Old Testament sacrament of consecration, would be spiritually actualized by the power of God (*cf.* 10:16; Jer. 31:33ff.; 32:39ff.; Ezek. 11:19; 36:26f.).

As the development of this theme in the prophets shows, the renewal and restoration which Moses foretells is that ac- complished by Christ in the New Covenant. The prophecy is not narrowly concerned with ethnic Jews but with the covenant community, here concretely denoted in its Old Testament identity as Israel. Within the sphere of the New Covenant, however, the wall of ethnic distinctions disappears. Accordingly, the Old Testament figure used here of exiled Israelites being regathered to Yahweh in Jerusalem (vv. 3b, 4; cf. 28:64) finds its chief fulfillment in the universal New Testament gathering of sinners out of the human race, exiled from Paradise, back to the Lord Christ enthroned in the heavenly Jerusalem.

Turn thy captivity (v. 3a), or "turn thy turning," refers to a radical change of condition. *The Lord thy God will make thee plenteous in every work of thine hand* (v. 9). Along with the spiritual gifts of regeneration, conversion, and sanctification by which the rebels would be transformed into faithful servants, the Messiah would give them a new world of prosperity and peace as their inheritance (vv. 3a, 5, 9; cf. 28:4, 62). The restored theocratic kingdom in Canaan is used as a typical figure for the antitypical reality, the eternal kingdom of God in the renewed universe which is the triumphant creation of Christ at his coming again in power. *The Lord thy God will put all these curses upon thine enemies* (v. 7). While the people of God inherit the earth, their enemies are to be plagued with every curse. The messianic salvation is thus a triumph of redemptive judgment, a new exodus and conquest, and therefore it is a renewal of the covenant mediated through Moses and Joshua, first at Sinai and afterwards in Moab and at Ebal and Gerizim.

E. RADICAL DECISION, 30:11-20

The section of the treaty concerned with covenant ratification (chaps. 27-30) closes with the call for decision, in which Moses reminds Israel that they cannot plead ignorance of God's demands (vv. 11-14) and warns them that the alternatives set before them in the covenant curses and blessings are those of life and death (vv. 15-20).

30:11-14. *For this commandment which I command thee this day, it is not hidden from thee, neither is it far off* (v. 11). The Lord did not require of Israel something incomprehensible or unattainable. Israel's duty was not hidden at some inaccessible height (v. 12) or beyond some insuperable barrier (v. 13). Note Paul's similar use of these proverbial questions in Romans 10:5ff. *The word is very nigh unto thee, in thy mouth, and in thy heart, that thou mayest do it* (v. 14). There are the secret, incomprehensible things which belong to God (*cf.* 29:29a; Ps. 131:1), but the covenant demand is one of the revealed things given to God's people to be obeyed (*cf.* 29:29b; 6:6, 7; 11:18, 19; 31:19). As Job affirmed, exhaustive knowledge is the possession of God alone, but to man God assigns as his portion of wisdom the fear of the Lord, which is the way of the covenant (Job 28, esp. v. 28).

30:15-20. Moses concludes his setting forth of the covenant blessings and curses with an appeal of memorable simplicity and sublimity. He reminds Israel that in their experience as a kingdom, blessing and obedience would be inseparable, as would also rebellion and the curse (vv. 16-18). *See, I have set before thee this day life and good, and death and evil* (v. 15). The issue was clear and radical as life and death (*cf.* v. 19b). To love the Lord, obey him, and remain loyal to him — *that is thy life* (v. 20; *cf.* 6:1-5). *I call heaven and earth to witness against you this day* (v. 19, ASV and RSV). One of the standard divisions in the secular suzerainty treaties was that containing the invocation of the gods of the lord and vassal as the divine witnesses of the covenant oath. It is significant that the Deuteronomic treaty contains at least a rhetorical imitation of that feature (*cf.* 4:26; 31:28; 32:1). Yahweh was of course the divine Witness as well as the Lord of this covenant. Over and over again Moses traces the work of salvation which God was accomplishing through him to the covenant promises sworn unto Abraham (v. 20b).

V. DYNASTIC DISPOSITION: COVENANT CONTINUITY, 31:1-34:12

This final section of the covenant document has as its unifying theme the perpetuation of the covenant relationship. Of special importance is the subject of the royal succession, which is also prominent in the extra-biblical suzerainty treaties (*cf.* above, the introduction to IV. Sanctions). This succession is provided for by the appointment and commissioning of Joshua as dynastic heir to Moses in the office of mediatorial representative of Yahweh (chap. 31). The testamentary assignment of kingdom inheritance to the several tribes of Israel (chap. 33) reckons with the status of all God's people as royal heirs. Included also are two other standard elements in the international treaties. One is the invocation of covenant witnesses, here represented chiefly by the Song of Witness (chap. 32). The other is the directions for the disposition of the treaty document after the ceremony (31:9-13). By way of notarizing the document, an account of the death of Moses is affixed at the end (chap. 34).

A. FINAL ARRANGEMENTS, 31:1-29

A series of charges is given by Moses, all concerned with carrying on the covenant and its program: to all the people (vv. 1-6), to Joshua (vv. 7, 8), and to the priests (vv. 9-13). Then in a theophanic revelation at the sanctuary (vv. 14, 15) the Lord instructs Moses concerning a Song of Witness for future Israel (vv. 16-22) and also commissions Joshua to his imminent command (v. 23). Finally, Moses again commands the priests concerning the disposition of the documentary witness to the covenant and concerning the assembling of the people to hear the Song of Witness (vv. 24-29).

31:1-6. On Moses' age (v. 2a), *cf.* Exodus 7:7; Deuteronomy 29:5. *I can no more go out and come in* (v. 2). Though Moses was still competent in terms of individual daily life (*cf.* 34:7), he had lost the stamina necessary to shepherd the whole flock of Israel and in particular to lead the campaign of conquest lying before Israel (*cf.* Num. 27:16ff.). However, it is possible that the disability in view arose not from Moses' physical condition but

135

from the divine prohibition (see v. 2b), for the verb *yākal* may be used in a permissive sense (*cf.* Deut. 12:17). On verse 2b, *cf.* 3:23ff.; 4:21f.; Numbers 20:12. *The Lord thy God, he will go over before thee . . . and Joshua, he shall go over before thee* (v. 3). The Lord, with Joshua as his new mediatorial representative, would continue and complete in Canaan the conquest already successfully begun under Moses in Transjordania (vv. 3-6). With such leadership assured them, Israel must execute the mandate of conquest (*cf.* 7:1ff.) with strength and courage (v. 6; *cf.* vv. 7, 23; 20:3f.; 31:7, 23; Josh. 1:6ff.).

31:7, 8. At the command of God Joshua had already been ordained by Moses before Eleazar and the congregation as the new leader of Israel (*cf.* Num. 27:18-23; Deut. 1:38). *Moses called unto Joshua . . . thou must go with this people unto the land . . . and thou shalt cause them to inherit it* (v. 7). Repeating the promise of the divine presence (v. 8; *cf.* Josh. 5:13ff.) just made to all the people (vv. 3-6), Moses publicly charged Joshua to carry forward to completion the mission of conducting Israel into its inheritance.

31:9-13. Moses assigned the priests and elders the duty of regularly republishing the law of the covenant. The effect of this was to associate the priests and elders with Joshua in the responsibility of rule and in the esteem of Israel. More important, all the covenant people together with all human authorities in the covenant community were placed under the lordship of the Giver of the law. *Moses wrote this law* (v. 9a). This is a clear statement of obvious import for higher critical investigations (*cf.* v. 24). Though the writing is mentioned at this juncture, it is probable that the official covenant document, or at least the main part of it, had been prepared earlier. *And delivered it unto the priests the sons of Levi, which bare the ark of the covenant of the Lord, and unto all the elders of Israel* (v. 9). This delivery of the law to the priests and elders, if it is to be distinguished from that mentioned in verses 24ff., might be simply a symbolic transfer of the responsibility of enforcing the covenant law, as described in verses 10-13.

When all Israel is come to appear before the Lord thy God in the place which he shall choose, thou shalt read this law before all Israel in their hearing (v. 11). In the suzerainty treaties of the nations, directions were included for reading them to the vassal people at regular intervals, from once to thrice annually. In Israel there was to be a constant proclamation of the will of

Yahweh through the service of the cult and in time through the ministry of prophets. Parents, too, were charged with the faithful instruction of the covenant children in the commandments of the Lord (*cf., e.g.,* 6:7, 20ff.). Hence the septennial reading of the law to Israel (v. 10) at the feast of Tabernacles (*cf.* 16:13ff.) in the year of release (*cf.* 15:1ff.) was intended not as the sole means of teaching the people of Israel their covenantal obligations but as an especially impressive reminder, at this time of sabbatical renewal and consummation, of the need for an ever fresh self-consecration by the servants of the Lord if they would enjoy the consummation of the covenant's beatitude.

31:14-23. *Call Joshua, and present yourselves in the tabernacle of the congregation, that I may give him a charge* (v. 14). Joshua, like Moses (*cf.* Ex. 3:1-4:17) was personally commissioned by the Lord himself. That was the chief and stated purpose for the summoning of Moses and Joshua into the presence of the heavenly Suzerain, who then spoke with them face to face as a man speaks to his friend (v. 15; *cf.* Ex. 33:9, 11; Num. 12:5). The words of the divine revelation (v. 23) were simply a direct statement of the charge and the promise given mediately through Moses (vv. 7, 8) and a confirmation of Joshua's public ordination (Num. 27:18-23).

This people will rise up, and play the harlot after the strange gods of the land (v. 16, ASV). On this occasion the Lord also confirmed the dark prophecies Moses had been uttering of Israel's future infidelity and God's wrath against them (vv. 16ff.), and he directed Moses to teach Israel a song which would be a witness for him against them when they broke his covenant (vv. 19ff.). Because of the abominable rites of the Canaanite fertility cult which would ensnare Israel, their lusting after idol-gods, their spiritual whoredom (v. 16; *cf.* Ex. 34:15, 16), would involve carnal prostitution as well. The inclination to ignore Yahweh would be most evident when Israel had become secure and prosperous in their land of milk and honey (v. 20; *cf.* 6:10ff.; 8:12ff.; 32:15). *Then my anger shall be kindled against them in that day, and I will forsake them* (v. 17). Such would be the inevitable consequence of Israel's forsaking the Lord. Without God's protection the nation would fall victim to many evils and so be made painfully aware that God was not among them (v. 17b). Lest the Israelites should then recall the divine promise not to forsake them (*cf.* v. 6) and perversely impute unrighteousness to him, God appointed for them the Song of Witness. *Put it in their mouths, that this song may be a witness for me against the children of Israel* (v. 19). The song would place the promised blessings and the threatened curse in their proper perspective within the covenant. It would proclaim the perfect righteousness of God and convict Israel of the justice of their afflictions (*cf.* 32:4, 5). It was only because of the pure grace of God that Israel might even enter the land of promise, for the Lord was fully aware of the pride and rebellion in their hearts even before he led them across the Jordan (v. 21b). Verse 22 anticipates verses 30ff.

31:24-29. *That it may be there for a witness against thee* (v. 26). The treaty document was to be preserved by the side of the ark of the covenant as a complementary covenant witness along with the song (*cf.* vv. 9ff.). This requirement and the similar disposition of the two Sinaitic tables accorded with contemporary practice (see comments on 10:1-11). Possibly it was one of the priests into whose hands the Deuteronomic treaty was now entrusted (v. 25; *cf.* 27:14) who affixed the record of Moses' death, or indeed everything from this point to the end. This official may have had some further but minor part in bringing the rest of the document into its final form. In these instructions to the priests all the treaty witnesses are brought together. The Song of Witness about to be recited to assembled Israel included at the same time an invocation of heaven and earth as additional witnesses (v. 28b). The force of the witness was primarily against Israel in view of their foreseen provocations (vv. 27, 29). The foreknowledge of Moses is the result of the revelation of the foreknowledge of God (*cf.* v. 21).

B. THE SONG OF WITNESS, 31:30-32:47

31:30. According to Moses' directions (*cf.* 31:28), Israel was assembled and Moses together with Joshua (*cf.* 32:34), the old and new representatives of Yahweh, proclaimed the song (Deut. 32).

Chapter 32. In its general structure this poetic song follows the pattern of the Deuteronomic treaty. After the invocation to the witnesses to give ear (vv. 1-3), the covenant Suzerain is identified in preamble-like fashion as God of truth and as Israel's Father (vv. 4-6). Then the historical prologue of the treaty finds its counterpart in a recital of the special favor which the Lord had shown to Israel hitherto (vv. 7-14). Next, the treaty stipulations are reflected upon in the condemnation of Israel's rebellion against Yahweh in favor of new gods (vv. 15-18). The consequence of this covenant breaking would be the heaping of the covenant curses upon them (vv. 19-25). Yet, as is also asserted in the blessing and curse section of the treaty, beyond the final curse lies the prospect of covenant renewal accomplished through a redemptive judgment in which God would avenge his servants upon their enemies; such is the closing theme of the song (vv. 26-43).

In the sphere of international relations the defection of a vassal provoked what may be called a covenant lawsuit. The formal proceedings included a preliminary message of warning to the offender and then a declaration of the suzerain's judgment, announcing his intent to enforce the sanctions of the covenant to the utmost. The structure of these communications paralleled that of the original covenant document with such modifications as were necessary to transform the treaty into an indictment (*cf.* Part I, Chapter II, note 26). Thus, the message sometimes opened with an invocation of witnesses (*cf.* Deut. 32:1); interrogation in which accusation was implicit was conjoined to the survey of the suzerain's benefactions (*cf.* Deut. 32:6); a charge of infidelity accompanied the reminder of oath-bound duties (*cf.* Deut. 32:15-18); and the curses became an ultimatum or verdict (*cf.* Deut. 32:20ff.). Deuteronomy 32 is then Yahweh's covenant lawsuit against his ungrateful and unfaithful people, prophetically delivered through Moses, "the man of God" (see Deut. 33:1, "the man of X" being a title for the messengers of great kings). Peculiar to Yahweh's declaration of judgment, however, is the introduction of his promise of ultimate mercy and blessing.

32:1-3. Invocation of Witnesses. *Give ear, O ye heavens . . . and hear, O earth* (v. 1). The address to heaven and earth must be understood as a summons to them to be witnesses of the covenant, since Moses has just stated that precisely that was the purpose of assembling Israel to hear the song (*cf.* 31:28). The way of the covenant and the way of wisdom are united here as Moses identifies this covenant song as *my doctrine* (v. 2), or *my teaching* (RSV), a word common in the Wisdom literature. *Because I will publish the name of the Lord: ascribe ye greatness unto our God* (v. 3). The song presents true wisdom because its theme is the fear of Yahweh, great God of Israel.

32:4-6. Preamble. *A God of faithfulness and without iniquity, just and right is he* (v. 4, ASV). The song is a theodicy (*cf.* comments on 31:19ff.). With that in view, the identification of the Lord is in terms of his perfect justice. *The Rock* (v. 4). This epithet contemplates God as the reliable Refuge of his people (*cf.* vv. 15, 18, 30). The Hebrew *ṣûr* as thus used of God may derive from a root meaning "mountain" (*cf.* Ugaritic *gŵr*). In contrast to God's righteousness is the perversity of the Israelites, these "sons of God" (cf. vv. 6, 18ff.; 14:1; Ex. 4:22ff.) who were actually *his not-sons* (v. 5a, literally; *cf.* "not-god" (v. 21) and "not-people" (v. 21)). This introduces the main burden of the song, namely, that Israel's sin provided a completely adequate explanation of all the evil that would overtake them. *O foolish people and unwise* (v. 6). In keeping with the wisdom motif, sin is regarded as foolishness (*cf.* vv. 28, 29). *Is not he your father, who created you* (v. 6b, RSV). The reference is to the Lord's forming of Israel into the theocratic people by election and redemptive calling out of Egypt.

32:7-14. Historical Prologue. *Remember the days of old, consider the years of many generations* (v. 7a). The fact that verse 8 refers to divine providence as far back as the events of Genesis 10 and 11 explains the historical perspective of verse 7a. *When the Most High divided to the nations their inheritance . . . he set the bounds of the people according to the number of the children of Israel* (v. 8). As Paul teaches that Christ rules over all things for the benefit of his church, so Moses affirms that Yahweh took special interest in the geographical needs of Abraham's numerous seed in his providential government of all nations (*cf.* Gen. 10:32), for Israel was his elect people (v. 9; *cf.* 7:6; 10:15). According to a reading supported by the LXX and Qumran fragments, "sons of God" would replace "children of Israel" (v. 8). Those who prefer this reading appeal to the mythical tradition that El, head of the Canaanite pantheon, had seventy sons, and to the fact that there are seventy nations mentioned in Genesis 10; and they conclude that this numerical correspondence is referred to in verse 8. Similarly, Jewish commentators, following the Massoretic text, saw a correspondence of the seventy nations of Genesis 10 to the seventy Israelites of Genesis 46:27.

Having arranged for Israel's inheritance in Canaan from the

days of old, the Lord was in the days of Moses conducting them into the possession of its rich goodness (vv. 10-14). *He found him in a desert land, and in the waste howling wilderness* (v. 10a). The Lord, coming to seek and to save that which was lost, found homeless Israel helpless in the desert. *He kept him as the apple of his eye* (v. 10b). He cherished his people as jealously as does a man that which is most precious to him (v. 10b), or as an eagle cherishes its young (v. 11). These figures might be interpreted of the deliverance from Egypt as well as the guidance to Canaan. *The Lord alone did lead him, and there was no foreign god with him* (v. 12b, RSV). Since Yahweh was Israel's sole benefactor, their subsequent shift of allegiance to foreign gods (*cf.* vv. 15ff.) was manifestly without excuse. *He made him ride on the high places of the earth* (v. 13a). In Yahweh's strength Israel advanced in majestic triumph through Transjordania (*cf.* 2:31ff.) and over mountainous Canaan to feast on all the choicest offerings of field and flock (vv. 13b, 14).

32:15-18. Record of Rebellion Against the Covenant Stipulations. *But Jeshurun waxed fat, and kicked* (v. 15). As their Suzerain, Yahweh's primary demand was for perfect and exclusive loyalty. But like an unruly beast, Israel, fattened in its rich pasture, refused. *Jeshurun* (*cf.* 33:5, 26; Is. 44:2) is a name for the people of Israel which is usually taken to mean "the upright." Another suggestion is that Jeshurun is a hypocoristicon and is to be identified with the name Israel. In either case the name is here used reproachfully. In their arrogant contempt for the Rock of their salvation, the Israelites paid their sacrificial tribute to phantom no-gods. *They sacrificed to demons which were no gods* (v. 17a, RSV), gods from whom they had received nothing and of whom hitherto they had never even heard. So unspeakable was their ingratitude that they preferred such new god-kings to the Rock who had shown to them the love of both father (v. 18a) and mother (v. 18b).

32:19-25. Curses on the Covenant-Breakers. *They have moved me to jealousy with that which is not God* (v. 21). In the Sinaitic Covenant, attached to the stipulation forbidding rival image-gods, was the warning: "I the Lord your God am a jealous God" (Deut. 5:9; Ex. 20:5). God responds to unfaithfulness in the covenant relationship with something akin to the fiery conjugal zeal of a man whose spouse has been unfaithful (v. 21; *cf.* v. 16). The law prescribed death for the adulteress.

The covenant curses threatened Israel with extinction if she played the harlot with the no-gods of Canaan (*cf.* 31:16ff.). From the fire of divine jealousy there is no escape; it burns unto *the depths of Sheol* (v. 22, RSV), the place of the dead. Applying the *lex talionis* principle, God would incite jealousy in Israel by means of a no-people (v. 21; *cf.* Eph. 2:12). He would reject the chosen people which had rejected him (v. 19), remove his covenantal protection from them (v. 20a), and grant to a people that had not known his covenant favor to triumph over his *children in whom is no faithfulness* (v. 20b, ASV).

I will heap evils upon them (v. 23, ASV). In verses 23-25, the covenant curses, especially pestilence, famine, and the sword — the terrors which come with the climactic curse of siege and exile, are threatened (*cf.* chap. 28). In that exile would be the triumph of the no-people; by it, Israel would be removed from God's kingdom and become herself a no-people (*cf.* Hos. 1:9). In the further unfolding of redemptive revelation God was to promise a renewal of his mercy whereby the no-people would become again "my people" (*cf.* Hos. 1:10; 2:23), and Paul interpreted that as fulfilled in the coming of Gentiles as well as Jews into the New Covenant in Christ Jesus (Rom. 9:25, 26). In that connection Paul also gives a turn to the idea of Israel's jealousy at the favor shown by God to the Gentiles (see Rom. 11:11ff.; *cf.* 10:19). The Mosaic Song of Witness itself anticipates the redemptive mercy and blessing that lie beyond the predicted cursing of Israel (see vv. 26-43).

32:26-43. Blessings through Redemptive Judgment. Attention is now focused upon the enemy nation which would mercilessly smite both infant and hoary head (*cf.* v. 25). *Lest they should say, Our hand is high, and the Lord hath not done all this* (v. 27b). Because it was a foolish nation (v. 28; *cf.* v. 21b) it would misinterpret its victory over Israel and withhold from the Lord the honor due him (*cf.* Isa. 10:5ff.). In order to cut short the pride of the enemy and compel the praise of his own name (*cf.* v. 43), the Lord would limit the enemy's slaughter of Israel (*cf.* v. 26). From the viewpoint of the covenant curses, this would be a stay of God's vengeance against Israel. The preservation of a remnant from annihilation is thus rooted in God's jealousy for his own glory; at the same time the ultimate vindication of his people, which the preservation of a remnant provides for, arises from God's compassion for them (see v. 36). *If they were wise, they would understand this*

(v. 29a, RSV). The foolish enemy should have known that their easy victory over Israel, the covenant protectorate of the Suzerain of heaven and earth, must be due to his displeasure with Israel (vv. 19ff., 30). Verse 31 is a parenthetical interjection of Moses, enforcing the cogency of verse 30 by eliminating the possibilty that the enemy's god had wrought victory for him. On verse 31b, see Exodus 14:25; Numbers 23 and 24; Joshua 2:9, 10; I Samuel 4:8; 5:7ff.; Daniel 4:34ff. Furthermore, if the enemy were wise, *they would discern their latter end* (v. 29b, RSV). This theme is continued in verses 32ff. *Is not this laid up in store with me* (v. 34) . . . *to me belongeth vengeance* (v. 35). The enemy's arrogance would turn to trembling if they realized that Yahweh, the God of Israel, who had judged even his own people in fiery wrath, would certainly judge them also with strict justice (v. 34) for their depravity and cruelty (vv. 32, 33). The greatest evil of the enemy nation was the very fact that it was the enemy nation to the people of God. For though in this they were the rod of God's anger against Israel, their own motives and purposes were quite different (*cf.* v. 27b; Isa. 10:7ff.). For New Testament quotation of verses 35, 36, see Romans 12:19 and Hebrews 10:30.

For the Lord shall judge his people, and repent himself for his servants (v. 36a). God's judgment of the enemy would be an act of vengeance and vindication in behalf of at least the faithful remnant in Israel. So the song returns skillfully to its main theme of Israel and the covenant sanctions, and it intimates that ultimate blessing will follow the penultimate curse. *When he seeth that their power is gone* (v. 36b). It would be when his people were as helpless as when first he found them (*cf.* v. 10) that God would intervene in redemptive judgment. Forgiveness, however, would be granted only as his people were confronted with their sin (vv. 37, 38) and so were led to godly sorrow and repentance and to trust in Yahweh as their true and only Rock. *See now that I, even I, am he, and there is no god with me: I kill, and I make alive* (v. 39). Promising to come in judgment as the Saviour of his servants, the Lord identifies himself as God alone and absolutely sovereign (*cf.* v. 12; 4:35, 39; 5:6a; Isa. 43:11-13). *For I lift up my hand to heaven* (v. 40). As he did in the Abrahamic Covenant, so in this New Covenant the Lord adds oath to promise, swearing by himself, for there is no other (*cf.* Isa. 45:22, 23; Heb. 6:13), that his judgment will be terrible against those who hate him (vv. 41, 42; *cf.* v. 35; Isa. 63:1ff.). In verse 42, the third clause completes the first; the fourth, the second. The song concludes with the prospect of jubilation over the judgment of God which involves both retribution upon the enemy and expiation of all guilt within the kingdom of God (v. 43). Since *the nations* universally are called upon to participate in the joy of God's salvation, the horizon of this hope is clearly the messianic age, when all the nations of the earth find blessing in the seed of Abraham.

32:44-47. The commissioning of Joshua and the instructions concerning the Song of Witness were joined in the special revelation at the sanctuary (31:14-23), and significantly Joshua was associated with Moses in proclaiming the song to Israel (v. 44). Moses sealed the recital with a final appeal to the covenant community to cultivate in its successive generations fidelity to the covenant, which in its summarization in the song was a witness for God to Israel (v. 46). The conclusion to the sanctions (30:15ff.) is echoed in the warning that covenant keeping was a matter of Israel's very life (v. 47).

C. MOSES' TESTAMENT, 32:48-33:29

32:48-52. *Cf.* 3:27; Numbers 27:12-14. *That selfsame day* (v. 48). It was towards the close of the day of the covenant renewal ceremony (*cf.* 1:3-5; 27:11; 31:22). Moses at God's command must ascend *this mountain of the Abarim, Mount Nebo* (v. 49a, RSV), there to die: *And die in the mount whither thou goest up* (v. 50a). On Aaron's death on Mount Hor (v. 50b), see 10:6; Numbers 20:22ff.; 33:37, 38. On the sin which disqualified Moses for entrance into Canaan (v. 51), see 1:37; 3:26; 4:21; Numbers 20:10ff.; 27:14. The performance of this command is described in Deuteronomy 34:1ff.

Chapter 33. In the ancient Near East a dying father's final blessings spoken to his sons were an irrevocable legal testament, accepted as decisive evidence in court disputes. In the case of the biblical patriarchs the authority and potency of their last blessings derived from the Spirit of prophecy in them, speaking in the testamentary form (*cf.* the cases of Isaac, Gen. 27, and Jacob, Gen. 49). As spiritual and theocratic father of the twelve tribes, Moses pronounced his blessings on them just before he ascended the mount to die (v. 1) and thus his words constituted his testament. In so far as Deuteronomy was a dynastic guarantee, Joshua as Moses' successor was the heir of the covenant. It was also true, however, that all the Israelites were God's adopted sons and thus heirs of these blessings of God's kingdom which were being dispensed through his servant Moses. It is impossible simply to equate the covenantal and testamentary forms without a drastic impoverishment and distortion of the covenant concept. But to the extent that the blessings promised in God's redemptive covenant are not inheritable apart from the Promisor's death, that covenant does include as one of its features the testamentary principle. (See further, Chapter 2 above, especially pp. 40f.).

Moses' poetic testament contains three parts: an introduction, describing the glory of the Lord as he declared his kingship in the giving of his theocratic covenant to Jeshurun (vv. 2-5); the blessings of the tribes, these being in the form of prayers, doxologies, imperatives, and predictions (vv. 6-25); and a conclusion, extolling God, the majestic Protector of Jeshurun (vv. 26-29). (For a useful study of textual problems in this chapter and a new translation, see F. M. Cross and D. N. Freedman, "The Blessing of Moses," *Journal of Biblical Literature* 67 (1948), 191-210. It is their translation of verses 2d, 3 which is quoted below.)

33:1-5. *The Lord came from Sinai* (v. 2). The appearing of the Lord as King of kings to proclaim his covenant was in radiant, sunrise-like glory over the eastern mountains of the Sinai peninsula (v. 2a; *cf.* the similar poetic descriptions of the desert theophany in Judg. 5:4ff.; Ps. 68:7ff., 17ff.; Hab. 3:2ff.). In attendance upon the King at his advent was a heavenly host of *holy ones* (v. 2b, ASV; *cf.*, too, Ps. 68:17; Zech. 14:5; Acts 7:53; Gal. 3:19; Heb. 2:2). Probably nearer than the AV to the true sense of verses 2d, 3 is a recent translation: "At his right hand proceeded the mighty ones, yea, the guardians of the peoples. All the holy ones are at thy hand, they prostrate themselves at thy feet, they carry out thy decisions." As Yahweh's earthly representative, Moses gave his covenant with its kingdom promises to Israel (v. 4) and by the covenant ceremony Yahweh's theocratic kingship over Israel was ratified (v. 5). On *Jeshurun*, see 31:15.

33:6-25. Moses blessed the tribes of the sons of Jacob's wives first, then the tribes of the sons of the handmaids. Though Jacob announced first-born Reuben's loss of the rights of primogeniture, both he and Moses began their testaments with him (*cf.* Gen. 49:3, 4). *Let Reuben live* (v. 6). Moses prayed that Reuben not suffer tribal extinction.

Hear, Lord, the voice of Judah, and bring him unto his people (v. 7). The blessing for royal Judah (Leah's fourth son) is in effect the prayer that Jacob's prophetic blessing on him be fulfilled (*cf.* Gen. 49:9-12), that Judah be enabled to accomplish the kingly task of conquering the adversaries and thence return to his people to receive their obedience.

In the testament of Jacob, Simeon and Levi (second and third sons, respectively, of Leah) were rebuked and scattered in Israel (Gen. 49:5-7). Historically, Simeon was early absorbed by Judah (*cf.* Josh. 19:2ff.). Moses omitted Simeon from the separate blessings (the number twelve being then obtained by the bifurcation of the Joseph tribe). But he invested Levi's distribution through Israel (*cf.* Josh. 21:1-40) with a new significance. Upon this tribe was conferred the honor of the priesthood in the family of Aaron with its privileges of receiving special divine revelation (v. 8a), teaching the covenant law (v. 10a), and officiating at the altar (v. 10b). Levi had displayed the devotion to the Lord requisite for the priestly office in the testing at Sinai (v. 9; *cf.* Ex. 32:26-29). On the events at Massah and Meribah (v. 8b), the beginning and end of God's trial of Israel (*cf.* 8:2ff.), see Exodus 17:1-7; Numbers 20:1-13; Deuteronomy 6:16; 9:22; 32:51. *Bless, Lord, his substance, and accept the work of his hands* (v. 11). Levi's blessing fittingly closes with the prayer that his priestly ministry in behalf of the covenant people may prove efficacious.

Having dealt with royal and priestly tribes, Moses turned to Benjamin (younger son of Rachel). *The beloved of the Lord shall dwell in safety by him* (v. 12). To Benjamin was allotted Jerusalem on the border of Judah, site of the Lord's sanctuary and throne (*cf.* Gen. 49:27; Josh. 15:8; 18:16). The use of the term "shoulder" in the latter passages (RSV) to denote Jerusalem's elevated situation supports the view that the Lord is the subject of "dwell" in the last clause of verse 12. On *beloved*, *cf.* Jeremiah 11:15; Psalm 60:5.

Adjoining Benjamin in the blessing and in territorial inheritance was Joseph (Rachel's older son). The double portion, right of the firstborn forfeited by Reuben, was given to Joseph (*cf.* Gen. 48:22) in that his two sons enjoyed separate tribal status *The ten thousands of Ephraim . . . the thousands of*

Manasseh (v. 17b). Moses confirmed the pre-eminence which Jacob gave Ephraim over Manasseh (*cf.* Gen. 48:14ff.). Again like Jacob, Moses blessed Joseph with military power (v. 17) and abundance of the choicest gifts of the earth (vv. 13-16; *cf.* Gen. 49:22-26). The source of all Joseph's prowess and prosperity was in the *favor of him that dwelt in the bush* (v. 16, RSV; *cf.* Ex. 3:2ff.). A slight change in the text would substitute "Sinai" for "bush."

Zebulun and Issachar (sixth and fifth sons, respectively, of Leah) were united in their blessing (vv. 18, 19; *cf.* Gen. 49:13-15). Their special portion was to be the treasures of the sea secured apparently by trade with those laboring in and along the Mediterranean and the Sea of Chinnereth. Their inheritances were near but not on these waters (see, however, Gen. 49:13). Verse 19a seems to indicate that their commercial successes would be thankfully acknowledged in true worship.

Gad (first son of Leah's handmaid Zilpah) had chosen *a commander's portion* (v. 21a, RSV) for an inheritance in Transjordania, the firstfruits of the conquest (vv. 20, 21a). Then they faithfully joined their brethren in the conflict for their portions in Canaan (v. 21b). *Blessed be he that enlargeth Gad* (v. 20). Like Shem's blessing (Gen. 9:26), Gad's was couched in doxology (*cf.* Gen. 49:19).

In energetic strength the tribe of Dan (elder son of Rachel's handmaid Bilhah) would be like the lions of Bashan (v. 22; *cf.* Gen. 49:17). It was to the area of Bashan that an expedition of Danites migrated from their earlier territory on the southern coast (*cf.* Judg. 18).

The Lord's favor on Naphtali (Bilhah's younger son) was to be shown in the remarkable fertility and beauty of his inheritance, especially its southern portion on the shores of Chinnereth (v. 23; *cf.* Gen. 49:21).

Blessed above sons be Asher (v. 24a, RSV). This tribe of Zilpah's younger son was situated on Israel's northwest border, a fertile land adjoining Naphtali (v. 24b; *cf.* Gen. 49:20). Moses' prayer was that Asher's protection might be constantly strong (v. 25).

33:26-29. *There is none like unto God, O Jeshurun* (v. 26a, RSV). As in the introduction to his testament (vv. 2-5), so in its conclusion Moses extols the true Giver of the blessings which he bequeathed. On verse 26b, *cf.* Psalm 18:10; 68:33. *The eternal God is thy refuge, and underneath are the everlast-*

ing arms (v. 27a); *cf.* the Mosaic Psalm 90:1, 2. The establishment of the theocracy was celebrated in the introduction, but here the Lord is praised as Israel's Defender and Benefactor in the subsequent conquest of the enemy (v. 27) and settlement in the paradise land (v. 28). *Who is like unto thee, O people saved by the Lord* (v. 29a). The uniqueness of Israel's beatitude derived from the uniqueness of Israel's Saviour-Lord (*cf.* v. 26a). *Your enemies shall come fawning to you* (v. 29b, RSV). All must acknowledge the supremacy of the covenant people of Yahweh.

D. DYNASTIC SUCCESSION, 34:1-12

A testament is of force only after the death of the testator. So the Deuteronomic Covenant in its testamentary aspect (*cf.* comments introductory to chapter 33) would not become operative until the death of Moses. Only then would Joshua succeed to the role of vicegerent of Yahweh over Israel, and only then under the leadership of Joshua could the tribes, according to the declarations of the Lord, enter into their inheritance in Canaan. It was, therefore, appropriate that the Deuteronomic treaty should close with the record of Moses' death, which in effect notarizes the treaty. That the testamentary significance of Moses' death is in view is evidenced by the accompanying attention given to the land of Israel's inheritance and to Joshua's accession to the royal mediatorship of the covenant. Verses 1-8 record Moses' death and verses 9-12, Joshua's succession to Moses. The account resumes the narrative of 32:48-52.

34:1-8. *And Moses went up from the plains of Moab unto mount Nebo* (v. 1a, ASV). Moses walked alone the ascent of no return, away from the promised land to the top of the mountain ridge on the west of the plains of Moab, opposite Jericho, to Mount Nebo. *The Lord showed him all the land* (v. 1b). The panorama of Israel's sworn inheritance is described as it appeared looking first towards the northeast, thence westward and south, back to the plain stretching between Jericho and Moses. The *Western Sea* (v. 2, RSV), *i.e.*, the Mediterranean, lying beyond the hills of Judah, is not naturally visible from Nebo. On verse 4b, *cf.* 1:37; 3:26; 4:21f.; 32:52. Though not now able to enter the land, Moses beheld its northern mountain peaks, on one of which he, with Elijah, was afterwards to stand, speaking with the Mediator of the New Covenant concerning the exodus he must accomplish at Jerusalem before he might cross over into the heavenly inheritance (*cf.* Matt. 17:3; Mark 9:4; Luke 9:30, 31). It was necessary for Jesus to die before entering his rest because he was the true Mediator who came to reconcile his sinful people unto God. Moses must die without entering the typical rest because as the Old Testament mediator he had by official transgression disqualified himself from completing the mission which prefigured that of the sinless Son of God. Unlike Moses, who after his death was succeeded by Joshua (v. 9), the messianic Mediator would succeed himself after his death because it was not possible that death should hold him. *His eye was not dim, nor his natural force abated* (v. 7b). Moses, though 120 years of age (v. 7a; *cf.* 31:2; Ex. 7:7), did not expire of old age but by the command of God, who by his sovereign word creates and destroys (v. 5). On the location of Moses' burial (v. 6), *cf.* 3:29; 4:46. On its sequel, see Jude 9.

34:9-12. *Joshua the son of Nun was full of the spirit of wisdom; for Moses had laid his hands upon him* (v. 9a). Joshua had been ordained as the dynastic heir by the bestowal of the charismatic gifts of this dynasty, pre-eminently the gift of governmental wisdom (*cf.* Num. 27:18ff.; Deut. 31). *And the children of Israel hearkened unto him, and did as the Lord commanded Moses* (v. 9b). True to their oath of obedience to Yahweh's will, sworn in the Deuteronomic ceremony (*cf.* 26:17; 29:12), Israel assented to the accession of Joshua. Though successor to Moses, Joshua was not his equal. Joshua must discover the will of God through priestly mediation (Num. 27:21), but with Moses God conversed directly (v. 10; *cf.* Ex. 33:11; Num. 12:8). By the signs of victory over Jordan's waters and Canaan's hosts, Joshua was attested as the successor of Moses who had triumphed over pharaoh's hosts and the waters of the sea. But none was like Moses in the fullness of his revelation of the Lord's redemptive might (vv. 11, 12).